After Trewyn

Harry Diamond 1998

Peter Davies is a well-known writer on
modern British art. He is a contributor to
'The Independent' and 'St. Ives Times
& Echo'. He recently wrote for The
Dictionary of National Biography
(O.U.P.). His previous books include
'St. Ives Revisited', 'Arthur Ballard'
(Old Bakehouse Publications), 'Michael
Kenny Sculpture' and 'The Sculpture of
John Milne'.

For Maggie and Ben

After Trewyn

Peter Davies

Peter Davies.

Old Bakehouse Publications

First published April 2001

ISBN 1 874538 24 7

Published in the U.K. by
Old Bakehouse Publications
Church Street, Abertillery, Gwent NP13 1EA
Telephone: 01495 212600
Fax: 01495 216222
www.mediamaster.co.uk/oldbakebooks

Made and printed in the UK
by J.R. Davies (Printers) Ltd.

Acknowledgements

After Trewyn is not a book about Barbara
Hepworth or even about her legacy. While her
inevitable influence casts a shadow like a giant
tree across the careers of most of the sculptors
covered in this book, her former assistants
developed in entirely independent ways -
sometimes complementing sometimes
departing markedly from her style.

The book is essentially five monographs
on Denis Mitchell, John Milne, Roger Leigh,
Brian Wall and Keith Leonard. My thanks go
to Irving Grose of the Belgrave Gallery for
commissioning me to write a book *The
Sculpture of John Milne* (2000). I am also
indebted to him for agreeing to launch
exhibitions in his London and St. Ives galleries
to launch this book. I also thank all the artists
or their families, in particular Denise Mitchell,
Breon O'Casey, Peter Thursby, Cosmo
Rodewald, Victor Sayer, Stanley Sellers,
Nicholas Leigh, Tommy Rowe, Brian and
Sylvia Ward, and Charmian and Mark
Leonard. I am also grateful for help from
H.C. Gilbert, Adrian Mibus, W.H.R. Cayton,
Paul Mount, Peter Ward, Liam Hanley, George
Neubert, Brian Smith, Mary Lambert, René
Gimpel, Madeleine Canney and Colette Bailey
of R.S.B.S. I wish to thank Toni Carver, editor
of *The St. Ives Times and Echo* for writing the
Preface.

This book, which sorely needed writing,
fills a big gap in the booming area of St. Ives
art. All are neglected sculptors and have
suffered unfairly at the hands of the painters
whose work has proved more seductive to
conventional lazy taste.

The final chapter deals with sculptors since
the 1970s, some of whom did not work for
Hepworth. I am grateful to Breon O'Casey,
Gordon Allen, Ann Christopher and Peter
Thursby. Simon Bishop, designer of early
issues of *Modern Painters* magazine - before it
went to the *Diamond Dogs* - designed the
cover of this book. Valerie Lowndes
generously compiled the index. Finally I thank
the staff of the Old Bakehouse without whose
cheerful involvement this book would not
have materialised.

Peter Davies

Contents

Foreword 6

1 *Denis Mitchell:* A Consummate Craftsman 9

2 1979-93 18

3 *John Milne:* Beginnings 24

4 A Modulated Monumentality 32

5 The 1970s: A Plastic Austerity 42

6 *Roger Leigh:* The Architect Sculptor 53

7 *Brian Wall:* Three Dimensional Mondrians 63

8 A Natural Gravity 72

9 *Keith Leonard:* The Search for Essence 83

10 A Fusion of Intentions 91

List of Black and White Illustrations 105

List of Colour Illustrations 107

Index 108

Foreword

Beyond a casual interest, no one can seriously address the art and sculpture created in St. Ives without attending to a plethora of relationships. Between artists, potters and sculptors; between artists and each other, their families, lovers, dealers, galleries, the media, the historians, the writers et al. The great truth of St. Ives is that it is the most curious of phenomena - an Art Colony, a bustling, thriving mass of imaginative, creative activity that has been steering a successful course through its evolution for well over a century. From time to time, this truth has proved inconvenient for commentators and art administrators. It is far easier to sell the idea that the reputation of St. Ives (or indeed British Art) is dependent on a few great 'artistic geniuses'.

I understand the dilemma. You can easily appreciate a worker bee collecting honey, but you keep your distance from the swarm! However, if the cause of art is to be advanced to the wider general public it is often necessary to focus a bright spotlight on one or two artists, presenting them for public attention, rather than attempt to explain the mechanics of the hive. Among the artists and sculptors of the St. Ives Modern Movement the need for the public to focus on the 'leaders' was very well understood. Essentially, it was this that lay behind the infamous split between the young artists (led by Ben Nicholson and Barbara Hepworth) and the traditionalists of the St. Ives Society of Artists in 1949. It was also what the foundation of the brilliantly successful Penwith Society of Arts was all about. It was an issue not only well understood by Nicholson and Hepworth but equally well by those who came to be dissenters: Peter Lanyon, Sven Berlin, Hyman Segal and Isobel Heath.

While this dispute is not the theme of Peter Davies' desperately needed and highly commendable *After Trewyn*, it is wise to understand the thinking of the protagonists. Coming from a well established and talented artistic family, art was the Nicholson's family business so he understood the need to promote his work, ideas and the modern movement. Like most artists I am sure he would rather not have had to bother but it was a job he knew how to do, and very well. Today, even though we hate 'spin' we do understand the absolute necessity for marketing. In 1949 St. Ives, however, there was a much higher 'integrity threshold' that the Penwith Society's dissenters were not prepared to cross. A degree of manipulation, dishonesty and ruthlessness was detected in 'hyping' modern abstraction over and above other forms of art and craftsmanship. For Berlin, a sculptor himself, the full implications of the Nicholson marketing strategy came when he mistook some Barbara Hepworth sculptures for those of Henry Moore, allegedly, to be told by Nicholson: 'No Sven, they're Hepworth's. Hepworth is to be the sculptor of the twentieth century.' And, let's face it, with a little help from her friends, pupils and assistants, (Henry Moore excepted) she was.

Those who perceived a degree of ruthlessness in the art politics that gave The Penwith Society the power needed to put avant-garde British Modern Art (not to mention St. Ives) back on to the international circuit were undoubtedly correct, there were losers. There was a price to pay. However, Ben and Barbara were first rate generals. The end result of the battle was that a large number of painters and sculptors became established in their own right and, frankly, there had been relatively few casualties. For its artistic leaders could St. Ives have done better? I think not. Dame Barbara particularly, came to display an extraordinary affection for her adopted town, a contribution recognized when she was made one of the last Freemen of the old Borough of St. Ives. As well as being one of the two most celebrated British sculptors of the century she became the best 'ambassador' St. Ives has ever had.

Although I knew both Nicholson and Hepworth I was far too young to claim any friendship. But of the 'younger' sculptors, both as a young and older man, I had several highly rewarding friendships with the great lady's former pupils and assistants. When my parents moved to St. Ives in 1951, having bought *The St. Ives Times*, their first Cornish home was a building at the back of *Trewyn* that had no name. My father sought the advice of a member of the St. Ives Old Cornwall Society, Mr. Stanley Cock, who suggested *Hanter Chy* - in Cornish literally 'Half a House'. We moved from here in 1957. A few months after John Milne moved into *Trewyn*, the front half of the building which adjoined Dame Barbara's famous *Trewyn Studio*. Much later, as a young man I visited John for the purpose of servicing his typewriter. From these few occasions I would take away knowledge and advice, generously given as a reward for a simple expression of interest in his work. Although he survived his famous tutor by a couple of years, John died tragically in 1978 at the early age of 47 and is often remembered and still missed in St. Ives to this day. It has been very good indeed to see the recent revival of interest in John Milne and his work and gratifying that Peter Davies has already published his book *The Sculpture of John Milne*.

My fondest memories of a Hepworth assistant are of Denis Mitchell. Mitchell is also by far and away my favourite sculptor. This is not to imply any usage of those meaningless generalisations of 'good' or 'bad.' I simply know the elements, form and elegance of line that are common to an aesthetic Denis and I shared about the landscape of West Cornwall. A song we both know so well but that only Denis could sing. If you could survive his robust 'mateship' which usually meant a double whiskey in your morning coffee when you visited! The wisdom and advice on offer, so generously made available was staggering. He was a fine sculptor, the most amusing of companions and a great man. His first-hand knowledge of everybody in the Art Colony from the 1930s onward was encyclopedic, 'All sealed in an envelope in the bank - to be opened fifty years after my death.' He would often joke with a wink and a chuckle.

It was indirectly through another former Hepworth assistant, Keith Leonard, that I first got to know the author of *After Trewyn* properly, although we had had a nodding acquaintance for several years previously. I had known and admired Leonard's work for many years. My first in-depth conversation with Leonard occurred when he popped into our office for some photocopying. A devout Christian Scientist and a self-effacing man of almost painful modesty he was genuinely shocked to discover that I knew who he was and that I liked his work. His sculpture, ultra-modern often celebrating dance and movement and always aiming for spiritual purity was very different from that of Denis Mitchell's. Different from the work of John Milne, Roger Leigh, Brian Wall or any other Hepworth assistant. There were no pastiche merchants or copyists to come out of the Trewyn Studio. Only good, clear thinking, original sculptors.

And, once again with Keith, that remarkable generosity - free with advice, free with information and often expressing far more interest in my work than wanting to talk about his own. It was on Keith Leonard's memorial retrospective exhibition catalogue that Peter Davies and I first worked together, along with my friend Dr. David Brown, the Tate curator responsible for the Tate (Millbank) *St. Ives 1939-64* show of 1985. Peter aptly entitled his article on Leonard, *'A modest man beyond the frontiers of academic practice'* a headline, which caught the man to perfection. Keith's wife Charmian epitomized her husband in a way no one else could have: 'Sublime purity was his concern, a view which may not be widely accepted, it was Keith's reality. Facially he shone with an inward glow of happiness and kindness which he liberally shared with all those with whom he was communicating.'

Those who know Leonard's abstract work sometimes feel that he achieved a more consistent purity of abstract expression in his work than Nicholson. But it was Nicholson's *White Reliefs* that reached the summit first. It was Nicholson who set the standard even if, arguably, he never quite managed to sustain it. Dame Barbara may have regretted missing a certain degree of elegance in her work captured by some of her assistants. But where did the generosity of spirit so evident in Milne, Mitchell and Leonard and which has been my lifelong experience of The St. Ives Art Colony come from, if not from the attitudes of their mentors? Of course there is the occasional buzz in the hive: a fuss, a fight, a bit of blather and squawk! But, essentially it is all part of the vital creative process that forges good human beings.

The evidence of Hepworth's success as a tutor, guide and mentor is self-evident in *After Trewyn*. Not before or since has St. Ives seen an enterprise like Hepworth's Trewyn Studio and in *After Trewyn* we see her assistants becoming fine and celebrated sculptors on their own terms with their own national and international reputations. A quarter of a century after Hepworth's death, Peter Davies gives us an extensively researched work which traces the careers of the 'once were' Hepworth assistants. The spotlight has been switched off and for the first time a broad beam illuminates an   exciting cast. Through their histories we reach a much better under-standing of what St. Ives is all about. Artists in community, learning from each other, creating great work while generally living together in harmony, sometimes with just enough discord to provide a very necessary cutting edge.

Toni Carver
Editor The St. Ives Times & Echo

Denis Mitchell in his studio with *Skiddaw* (1974). To the right is the large elm carving *Geevor* (1961).

1

Denis Mitchell:
A Consummate Craftsman

Denis Mitchell (1912-1993), who grew up in Swansea, spent all 63 years of his adult life in Cornwall. He practised as a sculptor for 45 of them. The longevity of his association with Cornwall out-stripped that of most of his contemporaries, who either came to Cornwall later or left before the conclusion of their careers. A Cornishman by adoption rather than birth, Mitchell lived through a period of great change, not only in the local art scene but in the social and economic conditions of west country life. He witnessed the replacement of inter-war landscape impressionism as the official St. Ives style (at least as far as the walls of the Royal Academy were concerned) with the abstraction of modern art. In the post-war period this became the recognised manner for which St. Ives artists became famous - or notorious - in London and beyond. For over a decade Mitchell became the principal assistant in the studio of the most famous of all those modern artists, Barbara Hepworth.

The use of Cornish place names with which to title many of his sparkling bronzes, refined wood carvings or clean cut slates - while providing a distinct aura of identification with the local landscape - is something of a misnomer. Mitchell's sculpture is not generally about landscape. In common with the sculpture of Moore and Hepworth the element of landscape is subsumed within a predominantly figure-based monolith. 'There is no landscape without the human figure,' Hepworth declared in 1952. More specific to the art of Mitchell, however, is a use of tall spiralling or streamlined shapes that refer to the tools of his trade. The sharp, jagged instruments of the agricultural labourer, the hooks of the fisherman or the power drills of the miner are recalled in the sculptural morphology of his mature work. And when, during the late 1940s, he relinquished work as a miner, market gardener and fisherman, he continued to use a wide range of chisels, hammers, drills and saws in the context of his new profession as sculptor assistant and sculptor.

To a greater extent than any other assistant, Mitchell's early progress as a sculptor was informed by the experience of carving out her designs. He had little artistic training before entering her studio, though had, for a number of years before the war, practised as a committed 'hobby' painter. In this his main subject was indeed landscape. The leisurely calm of pre-war Cornwall is conveyed. The pictures also contain a curious mixture of natural facility and naive stiffness, a product, perhaps, of a non-intellectual yet sagacious sensibility. The subjects are autobiographic, focusing on the people or places that meant most. A spate of self portraits was followed, after the bachelor's marriage to a St. Ives girl, Jane Stevens, in 1939, by portraits of his wife and, later still, of their young daughters. Other subjects to engage his attention also reflected a high degree of identification with things he came to know intimately. Several oils, depicting the tin mine at Geevor, near St. Just, where he worked for some years, or the quayside at St. Ives which he knew from the years on fishing boats, were a prelude to the almost fortuitous discovery of his true vocation as sculptor. Mitchell became the main professional assistant to Barbara Hepworth through the recommendation of Bernard Leach. The decade spent in her studio proved his real education as an artist.

It was not, though, until the second half of the 1950s that Mitchell found his voice as a fully independent sculptor. The few wood carvings produced during the early part of that decade do, however, manage to hold integral autobiographic content. In common with the paintings, Mitchell's early sculpture is a distilled expression of what was happening in his life. The stocky, yet intricate elm carving *Maternal Form* (1950) clearly reflected his life as a family man. The more abstracted *Family Group* (1954), a set of five wood rectangles mounted on thin tripods, does so to an even greater extent. During that year Judith, the third of his daughters, was born. The five geometric forms of the composition are therefore a symbolic ensemble relying for their effect on scale and disposition. During the period Mitchell made 'drawings' for sculpture, characteristically oils on gesso. By mapping out ideas for sculpture, these had crossed the aesthetic Rubicon, leaving behind the illustrated naturalism of early landscape painting and opting for the abstract shapes that would increasingly represent his mature sculptural language. The sculptural effect of these 'studies' was enhanced by a tactility of surface. This was achieved through scraping and incising a gesso ground, a technique no doubt learnt from Hepworth and Nicholson who used the manner to appropriate the faded grandeur of early Renaissance fresco painting.

By the mid 1950s Mitchell was slowly finding a formal language that was in part unique to him and in part derivative of Hepworth. In the early days of their 'partnership' Hepworth - whom Mitchell described as having 'the eye of a hawk' - worked alongside her assistant. He thus learnt through a direct observation of her working methods.Through this interaction an osmosis of idea and process inevitably took place. The question of influence is at best subjective and problematic. Though admitting that it was 'difficult not to be influenced by her', Mitchell was conscious of something different happening in the context of his own art. This seemed informed by fragments or partial elements picked up almost unconsciously during the process of working for another artist. 'As an artist,' Mitchell declared in a 1981 interview, 'you're really only interested in the artists you can get something from... the first thing you do may be very similar. And that will trigger you off in your own direction.' '[1]

Since Mitchell the sculptor was spawned entirely in the womb of the Hepworth atelier, the subsequent nature of Mitchell's formal development was predicated by a reaction to the Hepworth phenomenon and by assimilation of other sources that were, in varying degrees, common to both. The isolation of Cornwall before the new mobility of the 1960s and beyond - compounded by the dearth of books on contemporary art - restricted the choices. The successful colonisation of the locality by internationally significant modern artists ensured, however, that Mitchell was never confronted by a parochial or narrow scene. Restriction invariably becomes an artistic virtue, resulting in a tightening and perfecting of form and a consolidation of the moral integrity of the artist's vision. Brancusi, Moore and tribal sculpture were the non-Hepworth sources to impinge most directly on Mitchell's style. He kept tribal masks on the walls of his Newlyn studio and something of the sharp rising horns of these masks are detectable in many of his upright forms. What the critic Roger Fry described in his book 'Vision and Design' as the 'Negro Sculpture' [2] also informed the iroko carving *Arch Priest* (1958), a tall, slim, mask-like sculpture whose title alludes to ancestral associations. The lignum vitae carving *Inner and Outer Forms* (1956) depends for its effect on a more formal, 'architectural' dialogue between light and dark wood and between hoops rising up a tall Brancusi-like column.

Denis Mitchell exhibition, Flowers East, London March 1993. The three sculptures in the foreground are left to right: *'La Pietra'*, *'Mullion'* and *'Oracle'*.

A continuing dialogue between figure-based and autonomous geometric sculpture characterised an 'oeuvre' in which 'soft' carving and 'hard' construction yielded contrasting formal outcomes. *Oracle* and *Brass Construction* (1955), represented this dialogue, the former offering a swelling bulk of sweeping curves, the latter a deft symphony of planes and lines sandwiched within a shallow space. Both, however, owe a palpable debt to Hepworth, *Oracle* resembling the older sculptor's 'Single Form (Dryad)' (1946). The replication of a tall torso rising into a bulbous 'head' consigns Mitchell's work to a creative parody of the Hepworth prototype produced nearly ten years earlier. *Brass Construction*, in contrast, is more general in its reference to the geometric language of pre-war constructive art. Its flat, if free-standing, surfaces anticipate the importance of relief-making through-out Mitchell's career. The medium allowed the graphic organisation of flat slate or stone surfaces to extend into the third dimension through use of extraneous metals like copper, brass or stainless steel.

Metal, particularly polished bronze, provided the medium through which Mitchell established his identity as a sculptor. Mitchell's earliest bronze, *Zawn* (1958), follows Hepworth's first post-war casting 'Curved Form (Travalgan)' (1956). *Zawn* is the first of the thrusting mechanistic shapes that derive from drills and corkscrews. The narrow, spiralling aluminium column of *Zelah 1* (1961) and its shorter polished bronze successor *Zelah 2* (1963) make even more explicit use of the analogy with percussive implements. The highly reflective surface of *Zelah 2* (1963) announces Mitchell's meticulous and painstaking rendering of rough foundry casts through laborious filing, chiselling and polishing. This results in a contemplative object of poise and beauty, self contained yet open to its surroundings in terms of mirrored distortions. Mitchell learnt about the importance of precision and finish from Hepworth, who always insisted on hair-splitting accuracy in the final surface articulation. Many fundamental

Denis Mitchell exhibition, Flowers East, London 1993. *'Zawn'* is above left, *'Swanna'* centre and *'Endoc'* far right.

shapes recurring in differing variations throughout Mitchell's career were patented during the late 1950s and early 1960s. One is a characteristic 'U' or 'V' shape, often with one arm raised higher than the other. Many of Mitchell's sculptures, which are trophy-like, show a predilection for slim, frontal, relief-like formats. The upright is certainly a dominant feature and as such confirms the abiding, if residual, association with the figure. Hepworth's blue marble 'Bicentric Form' (1949) was instructive here, no doubt inspiring Mitchell's squat *Maternal Form* of a year later and providing a general prototype for many subsequent stylised abstractions of the figure.

A number of Mitchell's sculptures during the early 1960s do, though, opt for the horizontal inclination and as such invite landscape interpretations. This is true of *Landscape Form* (1960) and *Porthgwarra* (1961), a polished bronze and guarea carving respectively. Both forms, however, also evoke fish, the undulations of the former turning into a rising head, the sweeping profiles of the latter registering the unmistakeable eye and mouth of a large fish or dolphin. Mitchell's streamlined forms were invariably a hybrid of combined associations. Irrespective of vertical or horizontal orientation and of surface polish or patination, the end product always registered meticulous refinement and a high level of finish. The patient shaping of the material saw the artist in a temperamental and technical accord with the general feeling of timelessness in Cornwall, a timelessness where pebbles, boulders and other landscape objects have been gradually eroded through the hand of time. The classical refinement of Mitchell's forms embody a redolent romanticism.

During the 1960s Mitchell's sculpture continued its tripartite dialogue with wood, slate and bronze. Slate was the preferred material for the early reliefs.

'Zelah 2' (1963). Bronze.

The artist later carved solid blocks of this brittle material to create free-standing, multi-faced sculptures. When these materials co-existed in a sculpture they did so in a conventional capacity, slate forming the bases for many bronzes. A series of slate reliefs produced in 1961 incorporated thin bronze bars, inserted into linear grooves across smooth, dark surfaces. A number of early bronzes develop the characteristic 'U' shape announced in the elm carving *Geevor* (1961). The slim forked forms of *Porthcressa* (1961) and *Talland* (1966), for example, not only grew from *Geevor* but led, in subsequent years, to a variety of intricate re-arrangements based on the same simple, but distinctive, format.

The decade working for Hepworth undoubtedly provided insight into the machinations of the art world. He made influential contacts that proved useful when he branched out as an independent sculptor. During the 1950s his membership, and indeed chairmanship (1955-7), of the Penwith Society, together with his role as leading Hepworth assistant, helped secure some significant one-man exhibitions in London and the United States. These started in 1957, a year that seems to mark the end of his purely local reputation. The first solo exhibition, at the AIA in London, was followed, during the 1960s, with a string of exhibitions at prestigious locations like Waddington Gallery, London (1961), Devorah Sherman Gallery, Chicago and Redfern Gallery, London (1962), Bianchini Gallery, New York (1963), Arnolfini Gallery, Bristol and Marjorie Parr Gallery, London (1967) and at the Richard Demarco Gallery, Edinburgh (1968). By the end of this eventful decade Mitchell had carved a niche as a widely-exhibited second generation modernist St. Ives sculptor.

Despite these successes a livelihood from sculpture alone proved an at best precarious, and at worst impossible, business. In order to keep solvent Mitchell taught part-time at Redruth School of Art and at Penzance Grammar School, providing an all-important financial cushion between leaving Hepworth's employment and becoming a full time sculptor in 1967. The impressive exhibition curriculum vitae no doubt gave Mitchell the confidence to sculpt full time.

Considerable sculptural variety derived from the intricate rearrangement of a limited formal repertoire. The similar upright 'forks' of *Boscawen* (1962) and *Clowance* (1964), for example, were alternatively joined and left unbridged; the negative interior spaces thereby yielded a looped and open 'U' shape respectively. Scale also played a vital role in changing the effect of sculptures that were otherwise morphologically close. Large and small versions of *Zelah*, *Porthcressa* and later of *Carnelloe* posited different sculptural experiences. The broad correspondence that existed among certain works reflected shared conceptions intimately tied to the working process. Ideas were realised through the slow shaping of hard materials. The outcome was a truthful record both of the materials and of the manner in which they were fashioned. Patrick Heron, writing the catalogue for Mitchell's solo exhibition at the Marjorie Parr Gallery, London, in February 1969, concluded that 'a Mitchell can only come into existence at all under the direct physical touch of the sculptor's hands.' Heron also distinguished Mitchell's project from that of the then overwhelmingly fashionable mode of construction, an impersonal process that allowed a more cerebral, hands-off approach using prefabricated industrial components.

The decision to sculpt full time resulted in a bountiful output during 1968 and 1969, enabling Mitchell to show much new work at the Parr exhibition. No less than half of the 29 sculptures displayed that February - in bronze, aluminium and wood - were from the recent harvest. *Carngalver* (1967), a slim horizontal bronze form reminiscent of a blacksmith's anvil, continued to associate with labourer's implements and machinery. It did, however, depart from the predominantly vertical format of Mitchell's previous oeuvre. The same anvil shape had characterised *Carn* (1961) and would occur again in *Tumarco* (1970), a small compact bronze with a less horizontal inclination.

'*Carn*' (1961). Bronze.

The recent bronzes exhibited with Parr were therefore a testimony to the abiding importance of carving, as opposed to construction, at the heart of Mitchell's work. The sculptures, described by Heron as 'hand carved metal', were carved both before and after bronze casting, the artist spending hours laboriously filing and polishing rough foundry casts. The mixture of smooth, rough, polished and patinated surfaces that resulted added textural variety to a range of shapes that balanced symmetry with a feeling of unpredictable movement. The architectural symmetry of *Solaris* (1968), registered by a portal-like central arch pierced with three circular 'windows', was also able to embody a convincing level of poetic allusion. The surrounding hewn bronze 'halo' invested this memorable work with a compelling feeling of pagan mystery. The simple but fundamental geometric contrasts between, for example, curved and straight, rounded and flat surfaces animated sculptures like *Nanquidno*, *Kerris* and *Gorran* (1968), the former's oval interior void softening the straight edges and sharp points of an inverted triangle. The Parr exhibition also presented three recent wood carvings, a lignum vitae *Culver*, a guarea *Carnelloe* and a teak form *Carnmenellis* (1968).

In 1969 Mitchell moved with his family from St. Ives to *La Pieta*, a large house above Newlyn. Parr helped the Mitchells acquire it. Since 1967 he had shared a Newlyn studio, 'Trewarveneth', with John Wells. A former schoolhouse once used by the celebrated Newlyn painter Stanhope Forbes, 'Trewarveneth' was now owned by Wells. It provided both with an ideal secluded working environment. The premises provided the backdrop to 25 glorious years of sculpture-making. Mitchell's first decade in Newlyn was ushered in by new opportunities. In 1970 he went on a lecture tour of Colombia, teaching for a month at the University of the Andes in Bogota. In

1973 he became a Governor of Plymouth College of Art and Design. On the exhibition front he enjoyed two solo shows, one at the Parr Gallery in 1971, the other at the Oxford Gallery in 1972. A number of group shows, notably an Arts Council tour featuring 8 artists chosen by Bryan Robertson in 1971, helped consolidate Mitchell's position within a contemporary art context.

The South American trip was reflected in the titles, if not the actual forms, of several new pieces, among them the slim, needle-like *Cerrito* and the extended horizontal bronze *Cordoba* (1971). Not only in terms of textural or geometric contrast, but also of orientation and placement, Mitchell's sculpture extracted variety out of a limited repertoire. *Luxulyan* and *Restormal* (1970) are a pair of small circular bronzes, the former upright like a solar disc, the latter reclining like a landscape plateau on a squat slate base. A number of new bronzes at this time, while adhering to Mitchell's predilection for slimness and uprightness, also presented themselves like mysterious sentinals. The feeling that they are watching and surveying is enhanced by slits or small head-like cavities cut into the top. *Gurnic* (1970), *St. Merryn*, *Endellion* and *St. Kevern* (1971) share this direct stance but differ quite radically from one another in terms of their morphologically varied profiles.

The decisive axe-like incision into the top of *St. Merryn* alludes to the robust action of a sharp implement. *St. Merryn* also proved a forerunner to sculptures that incorporated shallow circular recesses into polished or patinated surfaces. The lyrical interplay between these different kinds of surface added textural variety of an almost graphic kind to sculptural form. The roles between opaque verdigris and reflective polish could be reversed, as in *Cauca* (1971), where sparkling surfaces lead the eye into a patinated notch-like interior. In *Trew* (1974), a small bronze that was a squared-off departure from *Solaris*, five ascending 'porthole' cavities added open space to the dialogue of variegated veneer. Other bronzes of the period, such as *Buryan*, *Pelyn* and *Carnelloe* (1975) continued to extend the contrast between open and closed surfaces.

Denis Mitchell bronzes. Left to right: *Endellion* (1971), *Carnelloe* (1975), *Polzeath* (1974), *Talmore* (1974) and *Pelyn* (1975).

By creating a pattern from solid form and void, as well as from an almost pictorial deployment of verdigris and polish, Mitchell's sculptures created complexity from simplicity. The negative shapes registered by displaced volumes added secondary imagery. In *Polzeath* and *Talmore* (1974) these voids created highly stylised images suggestive of keyholes or other mechanical channels. *Endoc* (1978), a striking circular slate form, was cut into with three such 'keyholes'. By making relatively minor variations to these formats a surprising morphological breadth was created among a body of work emanating from a similar set of forms. *Nansalsa* (1975), for example, looked a very different sculpture from its kindred *Nanquidno* simply by its use of a double rather than single, incision into the shared format of an inverted triangle. A slim lignum vitae carving *Argos* (1974) similarly departed from a small bronze form, *Paphos* (1974) by virtue of minor inflections of surface.

During the productive years of the mid 1970s, Mitchell turned his hand to carving slate. *Skiddaw*, *Coniston*, *Hellvellan* and *Stranraer* (1974), which use a mixture of Cornish and north country titles, reflect being carved in honiston, rather than local slate. Not long after, however, Mitchell turned to delabole, a north Cornish slate, out of which he fashioned *Gernoe* (1977) and *Endoc* (1978). The slate carvings in honiston and delabole made up the

Denis Mitchell
Argos (1974).

seven pieces exhibited in Mitchell's large retrospective at the Glynn Vivian Art Gallery in his hometown Swansea during the autumn of 1979. The easily fractured nature of slate required careful, even machine-precision, treatment. The clean-cut look of the slate sculptures are a reflection of this. By absorbing, rather than reflecting, light these sculptures relied on feelings of weight, volume and surface direction. The playful use of cavities and of various surface finishes in the bronzes was clearly not possible with slate, though in certain late slate reliefs Mitchell ingeniously inserted thin rods of metal in surface grooves. Slate indeed lent itself to relief-making, and Mitchell frequently created linear incisions to break up the dark anonymity of the flat plane surfaces.

In 1975 Mitchell turned 63. Although he later called the 1979 Swansea retrospective his 'retirement exhibition', Mitchell had reached conventional retirement age by the mid 1970s. Hepworth's death in 1975 seemed to symbolise the end of an era, bestowing upon Mitchell's subsequent output that of a standard bearer. Sales of work during the decade had vindicated the decision to sculpt full time. He enjoyed several significant solo shows, at the National Museum of Malta (shared with the painter Misome Peile) and at the Compass Gallery, Glasgow in 1973, at the Oxford Gallery in 1974 and at the Marjorie Parr Gallery in 1975. In 1976 he participated in a three-man show, with Barbara Tribe and Paul Mount, at the Newlyn Orion Gallery, to which institution he had been elected to the Council of

Management in 1974. In 1977 he became a Governor of Falmouth School of Art, confirming his status as a recognised member of the Cornish art establishment.

FOOTNOTES:

1. Denis Mitchell interview with Edward Robinson. 12/11/81.
2. Roger Fry. 'Negro Sculpture' p.99-103.
   'Vision and Design'. Chatto and Windus. 1957. (7th Impression).

1979-93

By the end of the 1970s most of the pioneering members of post-war St. Ives art still based in Cornwall - John Wells, W. Barns-Graham, Terry Frost and Patrick Heron - had entered conventional retirement age. But artists generally do not 'retire' and the 1980s proved an invigorating period of undistracted work. Denis Mitchell was no exception. Along with the others a distinguished body of late work extended the achievements of early St. Ives modernism. At a time when the achievements of that earlier era had crystallised into history and was being reassessed as such, Mitchell and the others were producing fresh interpretations of old themes. Perhaps because sculpture could not be produced to a market demand as readily as painting, Mitchell did not succumb to the over-production that diluted the standards of some of the painters. This was no less true of Mitchell than it was of his close friend John Wells, whose output by the 1980s was negligible. This situation can, ironically, be read as a strength, an endorsement of Wells' integrity as an artist where idea and meaning was paramount. Mitchell himself struck a balance between the extremes of under and over production.

The large exhibition 'St. Ives 1939-75' held at the Tate Gallery, London in the middle of the decade was the culmination of this reassessment. Overshadowed by 'pop', 'post painterly abstraction' and finally 'minimalism' during the 1960s and 1970s the historical status of St. Ives as an important avant garde centre was now re-surfacing. As well as consolidating St. Ives's historical position, the 1985 Tate exhibition led to dramatic changes in the critical and commercial reputations of surviving or still productive St. Ives artists. The year 1979, a watershed in politics, saw the appointment of Alan Bowness, the art historian son-in-law of Barbara Hepworth, as the new Tate Gallery director. The re-evaluation of St. Ives art during the 1980s was therefore in safe hands.

While sales from Mitchell's large retrospective at the Glynn Vivian Art Gallery, Swansea, were disappointing, Mitchell's position within the loose grouping of St. Ives artists was assured. During the 1970s sales of Mitchell sculpture had largely come about through his able London dealer Marjorie Parr. Mitchell signed her copy of his Swansea

Denis Mitchell (left) with Mary Lambert, Marjorie Parr and Breon O'Casey. London early 1970s.

exhibition catalogue. 'You made so much possible for me and granted my greatest wish to live on my work,' he wrote on the inside catalogue cover in October 1979.

The early 1980s saw the recent septuagenarian continue to work energetically in a variety of materials. There is no sudden or marked diminution in either the quality or quantity of sculpture. The later works have a machine-like precision, not because they relinquish hand-made craftsmanship but because power tools and other technical aids are used. Nowhere is this clearer than in *La Pietra* (1986), an immaculately carved piece of gritstone that originated in a small earlier maquette. *La Pietra* was purchased by John Wells, who donated it to the Tate Gallery. The late bronzes have a similar elegant finish and are simpler than before. Often shedding the textural dialogue between high polish and verdigris, they opt for a uniform reflective finish. Shorn of superficial detail, these late bronzes are naked records of a streamlined formal conception, the product of virtuoso carving applied to both pre and post cast stages.

Many of these striking, sparklingly new later forms in fact derived from drawings Mitchell made over thirty years earlier. 'I start with my drawing,' he told Edward Robinson in 1981, as 'a sculptor has far more ideas than you'll ever produce.' [1] As his physical energies declined so Mitchell relied more and more both on a rich stock of earlier graphic plans for sculpture and on the trusted hands of his long standing friend and studio assistant Tommy Rowe. Rowe recalled that 'Denis wasn't doing a lot of work' [2] by the late 1980s. Often the shape for a new sculpture would be chosen from an old sketchbook; from it Rowe worked up a plaster model under Mitchell's direct supervision and, once approved and cast at the foundry, would be chiselled and filed into an immaculate, sparkling metal form.

The late sculptures form a morphological continuum with earlier work. *Traeve* (1992) derived, not from a drawing but from the backbone of a turbot that Rowe, a part time fisherman, salvaged and showed Mitchell. The older man mounted the 'objet trouvé' and later instructed Rowe to build a plaster, leading to a notable bronze sculpture that, despite its literal interpretation of a natural form, functioned as an intriguing and mysterious abstract shape. *Trellisick* (1988) an upright polished bronze of similar height, reverted back to earlier sketchbooks and, in particular, to a series of works announced in the *Zelah* series. *Trellisick* used angular rather than spiralling movements. *Trewarveneth* (1992)

Tommy Rowe working under Denis Mitchell's supervision, Newlyn early 1970s.

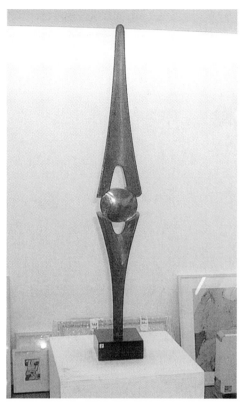

Mitchell's last significant sculpture, adapted the slow upward movement of *Trellisick* to the rotating rhythm of *Zelah*. Again adapted from an early drawing, 'Trewarveneth' is one of Mitchell's finest bronzes possessing the exhilarating upward thrust that characterises Mitchell at his best. The artist was justly pleased with the outcome.

In similar fashion, the slate sculptures of the last years echoed earlier forms, particularly bronze sculptures. *Carncrows* (1981) *Poljigga* (1990) and *Nanjivey* (1991), each carved in delabole, closely echoed the rounded rectangle, bisected sphere and diamond formats of *Verryan* (1975), *Poldu* (1980) and *Gwennap* (1968) respectively. *Zennor Head* (1985), by contrast, was a delabole carved by Rowe from an earlier, and smaller, version in honiston slate. Both the large *Zennor Head* and *Endoc* were carved from a large piece of delabole retrieved from an old billiards table. There was something very Cornish in such makeshift use of discarded materials close to hand. On a conceptual level, too, Mitchell turned to what was at hand in the way of provisional drawings made many years before. He admitted in the 1981 interview that 'I do go back to things I've done before and feel I could now do a better one slightly different'. [3]

In spite of the industry of Mitchell's so-called 'retirement' period, the early 1980s proved a quiet one on the exhibition front. It was not until the middle of the decade, with an appearance in the large Tate Gallery exhibition in February 1985, followed by a full airing at the Newlyn Orion Gallery, that Mitchell's recent endeavours were accorded due public recognition. While this solo show was retrospective in character - the superb early guarea carving *Porthgwarra*

Above Left: Traeve (1992) Bronze.

Above Right: Denis Mitchell with 'Zennor Head' (1985) Slate.

Right: Denis Mitchell. *Trewarveneth*. 1992.

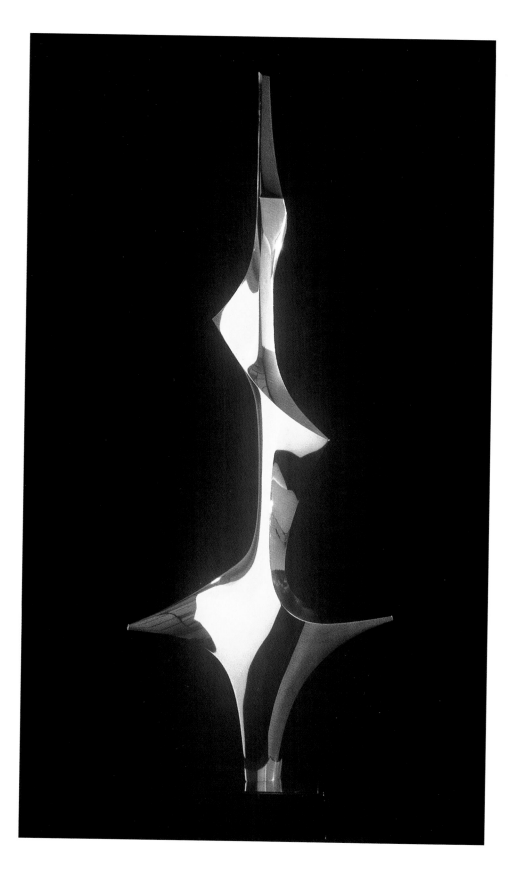

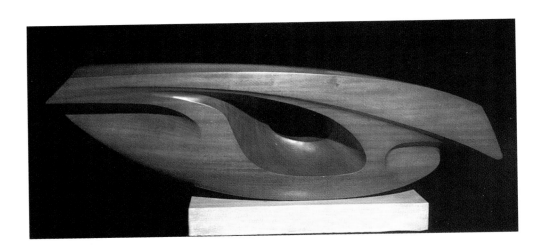

Above: *Gemini* (1973) Marble.

Top: Denis Mitchell. *Porthgwarra*. 1961.

Bottom: Denis Mitchell. Collection of bronze sculptures.

was something of a yardstick against which recent carvings could be measured - enough new work was displayed to suggest the undiminished productiveness of his enterprise. A group of recent lignum carvings, *Bodrean, Bolingey* and *Blisland* (1985), together with a yew sculpture *Roseveor* (1985), bore this out. In common with the late 'oeuvre' these carvings developed earlier forms, the serrated edges of *Blisland* recalling the early iroko *Arch Priest*, the opened cylindrical column of *Bolingey* owing a debt to the large marble *Gemini* (1973), the swollen column of *Roseveor* bearing kinship to *Argos*. The 1985 carvings also echo one another, an idea from one piece feeding into and generating a new form in a kindred sculpture.

The carvings in both wood and slate from 1985, a particularly fertile year undoubtedly stimulated by the Tate Gallery exhibition as well as by thoughts of a large solo exhibition on home soil, were in large part executed to Mitchell's directions by Rowe. The lignum vitae was a material that had been lying around the studio for many years. Originally acquired by John Wells and Mitchell from an ex-government surplus store in Hayle, the wood was transformed from naval to artistic purposes. The prominent sub-strata veining, by investing dense material with a quality of transparency, mitigated the rigidity of the imposed design while registering unpredictable features. The dark anonymous surfaces of contemporary delabole slate sculptures like *Tresco* (1984) and *Carnon* (1985) also threw up antediluvian patterns, a prominent streak of veining running below the central circular depression of the former and diagonally across the upper portion of the latter. Both sculptures stand upright like memorial stones. Together with the striking pierced slate form of *Zennor Head* (1985) these new slate sculptures were included in the Newlyn exhibition.

The collective and individual esteem generated by the 1985 Tate Gallery exhibition saw further exhibition opportunities for Mitchell during the latter years of the 1980s. In October 1986 he exhibited at the Crane Kalman Gallery, London, alongside

Right: *Tresco* (1984) Slate.

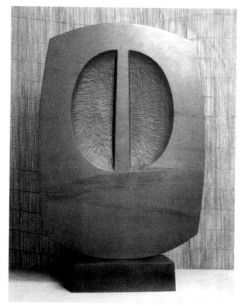

21

paintings by Patrick Hayman. The naive and expressionist qualities of Hayman's work complemented the quieter, more implicit, primitive character of Mitchell's sculptures. In 1990 Mitchell exhibited again with a respected London gallery, that of Gillian Jason. His work was also displayed in several notable group exhibitions, among them Newlyn Orion's touring display 'Looking West' (1987); Cornwall County Council's centenary exhibition in Truro, 'A Century of Art in Cornwall'; and a three-man show at the Berkeley Gallery, London, shared with Terry Frost and Tony O'Malley.

Although his health was declining, the early 1990s saw Mitchell preparing for two sizeable solo shows in 1992 - an 80th birthday exhibition at the Penwith Galleries in June and a display of work from the 1980s and 1990s that ran at Falmouth Art Gallery from mid September to mid October. While he seldom mixed materials in any individual sculpture - other than mounting a cast form on a stone or slate base or inserting thin metal bars into vertical surface grooves of slate - both exhibitions confirmed the artist's ability to pursue kindred ideas in a wide assortment of materials. *Thrust 11* (1992), a tall, pointed bronze form that was based on an old sculpture originally cast in aluminium, showed Mitchell traversing materials in the pursuit of a single sculptural idea. The bronze was exhibited at Mitchell's final lifetime exhibition in March 1993 at the Flowers East Gallery, London, from where it sold. The shape, which developed from a hook-like crescent into a tapering vertical column,exemplified the critic Richard Walker's earlier description of the 'slim grace of Denis Mitchell's forms'. [4]

The large Penwith exhibition - comprising 80 pieces of sculpture or relief and many drawings and paintings from both the early representational and the mature abstract 'oeuvre' - was accompanied by a sizeable catalogue. Introduced by Newlyn Orion's director John Halkes, the catalogue contained 7 tributes from colleagues like Roger Leigh, Breon O'Casey, Michael Snow and Terry Frost. Reflecting Mitchell's popularity within a tight knit, if fractious, artistic community, these tributes also pinpointed a sculptor craftsman's unique contribution. Leigh's assessment, by a sculptor who not only worked alongside Mitchell

in Trewyn Studio but succeeded him as Penwith chairman, had a telling ring. Mitchell was, Leigh considered, Hepworth's 'buttress'; and as Penwith Society chairman he was 'diplomatic, sensitive and considerate,' [5] qualities needed to steer the dissension-racked organisation through some torrid times.

Denis Mitchell preparing an exhibition at Marjorie Parr Gallery, London, early 1970s.

The slim elegance and unblemished finish of the late bronzes owed much, not only to final studio refinement but also to the excellence of a local foundry, Tyrrells in Hayle, where most of the later Mitchell's were cast. The firm returned quality castings less 'potmarked' with cavities, air pockets or other surface inconsistencies. It was at this foundry that enough late castings of Mitchell's sculpture were made to keep Rowe active, finishing off work several years after Mitchell's death. Rowe mounted Mitchell's final exhibition at Flowers East in London, an exhibition that Mitchell was unable to attend but about which he was excited.

The tradition of modern sculpture to which Mitchell's work belongs envisaged form through an unsullied union of conception and craft. Like a primitive labourer the artist realised his or her vision through an intimate accord both with the materials at his disposal and with the way they were fashioned. Whether or not the artist worked to pre-designed or open-ended strategies the process of making the free-standing object was registered in the final outcome. In Mitchell's case the subject, as well as the means, identified with the implements of his trade as sculptor, and before it, as fisherman or agricultural labourer. The peasant folk and tribal traditions that had inspired Brancusi, Hepworth and other distinguished predecessors once again proved relevant. If the use of Cornish titles provided only a superficial association with Cornwall then the pointed, hook-like shapes of many of his sculptures identified strongly with traditional Cornish industries such as mining, fishing and quarrying.

Mitchell's death, merely weeks before the opening of Tate St. Ives, denied a stalwart a part in the lavish celebrations that attended its mid-summer opening. During most of the time since June 1993 however, the gallery has displayed at least one of Mitchell's forms. The curatorial pairing of his bronze *Turning Form* (1959) with John Wells's lithe, aerodynamic composition 'Aspiring Forms' identified not only a long friendship but a shared aesthetic programme capable of traversing different media and two and three dimensions. *La Pietra*, Wells's gift to the Tate, was another Mitchell displayed at the Porthmeor gallery. At the time of writing, however, Tate St. Ives has not extended to Mitchell the honour of a retrospective exhibition that it gave Wells in 1998. A memorial exhibition of Mitchell's work was instead mounted by the Glynn Vivian Art Gallery in 1994. A celebration of Mitchell's achievement fifteen years after his earlier retrospective in Swansea, the exhibition confirmed conceptual integrity, consummate craftsmanship and mastery of small, medium and large scale as qualities at the heart of his work.

FOOTNOTES:

1. Interview with Edward Robinson. 12/11/81.
2. Tommy Rowe in telephone conversation with the author. 9/8/00.
3. Denis Mitchell interview with Edward Robinson. 12/11/81. Courtesy Mary Lambert.
4. Richard Walker. Review of St. Ives Group exhibition at Austin Reed Gallery, London. 'Arts Review'. 28/9/68.
5. Roger Leigh. 'Denis Mitchell Sculptor'. Catalogue for exhibition at Penwith Galleries. June 30-Aug. 1 1992. p.28.

3

John Milne: Beginnings

The sculpture of John Milne achieves an elegant poise at variance with the tension and turmoil behind its creation. Towards the end of his life Milne wrote that his drawings, always a vital creative accompaniment to three dimensional work, 'still reflect a terrible struggle but the delineation, and sometimes even the forms, reflect serenity and ease.' [1] In common with other young sculptors who assisted in Barbara Hepworth's Trewyn Studios at St. Ives during the 1950s, Milne went on to produce a sizeable body of work, wilfully independent yet stamped with the imprint of Hepworth's modernist workshop. The sharp, pointed features that occur in his sculpture are more a geometry of balance than a geometry of fear. The delicate surface rhythms and gently swelling forms in many of his best pieces contrast with the geometric symmetry and spiralling movement characteristic of Hepworth. Milne in fact looked as closely at Brancusi as at Hepworth and appropriated specific architectural source material, factors that serve to identify his work as standing on its own terms within the modern movement in St. Ives.

Although he shared with Hepworth an abiding interest in landscape, translated with imaginative daring into the conventions of monolithic modern sculpture, Milne adapted shapes derived from personal experience of exotic cultures. The unmistakeable wavy rhythms of Moroccan deserts or of Greek mountain ranges, together with ancient edifices, inform much of the later sculpture. In other sculpture Milne followed Hepworth in using Cornish themes, yielding images based on pebbles, waves and standing stones. It is, however, probably fair to say that the younger artist most effectively moved from under her shadow by replacing her correspondence between figure and landscape with a tie-up between architecture and sculpture. He thought in terms of architecture and managed to integrate the two in the particular instance of the bronze relief, a medium in which he excelled.

One of Milne's best known and most prominent sculptures, *Megalith II* (1974) possesses the frontal flatness of a relief. Placed in Trewyn Gardens, St. Ives, *Megalith* is a memorial to Hepworth. The only instance of a sculpture, other than by Hepworth, publically sited in the town, *Megalith* is a cogent and sad reminder of Milne's untimely death merely three years after that of Hepworth. As such it serves as a fitting monument to Milne's own notable achievement.

John Milne was born in Eccles, Lancashire in 1931. The youngest of six children, John was not encouraged by his father, a Scottish tailor, to pursue an artistic career. To appease career-minded parents he entered the Salford Royal Technical College to study electrical engineering, though succeeded in transferring soon after to the adjacent art school. He spent the next six years studying art, where a knowledge of engineering was not irrelevant. In the old pre-Coldstream Report regime, art students were required to learn a wide range of craft skills. Open experiment was discouraged. Different colleges did, though, excel in different disciplines and Salford, like many northern colleges, had an excellent textile design department. Sculpture hardly figured at all, a factor that confirms what must have been a marked determination on the part of Milne to specialise in 'three dimensional design'.

Milne's ambitions to become a sculptor were, however, helped by the college's pottery kiln, where he fired his earliest sculptures - small, distinctive, rotund figures vigorously modelled in clay. The stylisation of these early terracotta figurines, which are single or paired and often sitting, stemmed from an awareness of modernism and of modernism's antique and primitive sources. *Four Studies for Sculpture* (1947-8) and the glazed *Reclining Figure* (1950) recall Moore's family groups and fallen warriors. The early bronze *Girl* (1950), on the other hand, possessed a strong surrealist architecture, reminiscent of F.E. McWilliam. In their swollen, sturdy aspects other terracottas like *Study of two Female Figures* (1949), revealed links with the neo-classical figures of Maillol and Frank Dobson. The symmetry and static monumentality of these figures also owed something to Assyrian bas reliefs, Egyptian friezes, archaic Kouros figures and other classical architectural embellishments that Milne, courtesy of books and of the British Museum, was looking at and studying from an early point.

The surfaces of these early figures were a product of animated modelling rather than the smooth finish of carving. They have a consistent, churned 'skin', an evenly distributed manual texture that does not distort pre-conceived shape. The surface texture of figure and support is, however, tactile and visually arresting.

Several sculptures of the 1947-9 period have seat-like bases which double up as formal pedestal and as supporting 'furniture'. A typical 1949 *Seated Figure* was displayed in the Spring exhibition of the Manchester Academy at the City Art Gallery in 1951, marking an auspicious debut for a twenty year old student. The sculpture, placed at eye level on a tall plinth, stood out in a long established annual exhibition where sculpture was invariably an appendage to painting. A photograph of the exhibition shows the sculpture standing rather magisterially against an adjacent wall of worthy, if conventional, paintings, among them Kenneth Craddock and Emmanuel Levy portraits, street scenes and a St. Ives landscape by Harry Rutherford, the 'Sickert' of the Manchester art scene.

Within traditionalist parameters the Manchester Academy was, by this time, a melting pot of stalwarts and emerging young artists who, if not modernist, were replacing older values. Established names like Tom Dugdale, Henry Lamb and Charles Cundall found themselves surrounded by a group of younger painters, among them Lowry, Theodore Major and Alan Lowndes, who replaced old romantic subjects with a raw engagement with the stark reality of the industrial landscape. Milne always avoided such realist subject matter. He hated the grimness of the bleak industrial scene, pre-Clean Air Act, and resisted making depictions of it. An interest in myth and fantasy informed his early drawings and two early commissions, a relief for a Presbyterian church in Eccles and a relief for a Pendlebury school. In spite of an escapist streak, Milne's work always declared formalist intentions, his identity as an artist lying in abstract reduction rather than in mannerist detail or symbolic overlay.

A dislike of Lancashire's depressing climate and bleak industrial topography, did not prevent him enjoying Manchester's not inconsiderable cultural life, buttressed by a publicly-minded city council proud of its Victorian heritage. The splendid Town Hall housed murals by the Pre-Raphaelite Ford Maddox-Brown. Important exhibitions, including wartime work by Picasso, Henry Moore and modern Italian artists, were put on at the City Art Gallery, while the Whitworth Art Gallery pitched in with a significant display of German art. In the private sector much was happening, too, with an entrepreneur Margot Ingham running the Midday Studios and the Hungarian emigré, Andras Kalman, opening the Crane Gallery in 1949. Milne would later exhibit work with Kalman, who also went on to exhibit leading St. Ives artists, among them Hepworth and Nicholson.

Milne's appearance in the 1951 Academy exhibition and two commissioned reliefs announced the arrival of a promising local sculptor. He soon needed to look beyond Manchester, however, and, after meeting Cosmo Rodewald, Professor of Classical History at Manchester University, found the spiritual and material means with which to escape and fulfil a passion for ancient and exotic cultures. The subject matter of the commissioned reliefs pointed in the same direction. The religious commission, a terracotta *Christ Carrying the Cross* (1950) was a dense figurative composition within a simple architectural format, that of an arch. The school commission *Minerva* (1952) adapted a classical theme to the socially relevant theme of education. Minerva is crouched reading a book against a radiant sun. The subject is delineated within a neutral square format. Unfortunately, the mundane brickwork into which the cast stone image was set did little to enhance an early artistic achievement.

Milne met Rodewald through a French historian, André Bourde, and found himself in a congenial group of academics and intellectuals. The connection with Rodewald, which would be crucial and lifelong, played an important part in the furtherance of Milne's artistic ambitions, Rodewald encouraging him and underpinning that encouragement with generous financial help. According to Rodewald, 'temperamentally we were different... but we got on well.' [2] Rodewald's circumspect academic outlook no doubt tempered Milne's youthful, and at times naive, enthusiasm. Also in the circle were Mente Siroto, a local potter, and Kathe Schuftan, a German refugee whose expressionistic drawings, in the manner of Kathe Kollwitz, Milne admired. Schuftan's sudden death in 1956 prompted Milne to produce several drawings in her memory, one of which, *Crucifixion* (1956), alludes to Schuftan's direct and painful experience of the holocaust.

The exposure to a vital, if small, enclave of cosmopolitan scholars and artists encouraged Milne to visit Paris, still the art capital, if by now a diminishing one, of the world. The modern masters whom Milne admired, among them Brancusi, Giacometti, Moore, Rodin and Soulages, affected his work in various and not always obvious ways. 'No sculptor he admired as much as Brancusi,' [3] Rodewald recalled, and it was certainly the combination of primitive, folk and modernist impulses in the Romanian carver's sculpture that drove Milne to destroy his post-student terracottas, abandon academic modelling and seek fresh avenues such as direct carving in stone or wood.

A texturally explicit and energetic handling of charcoal, conté and other soft drawing materials emulated the gestural mark malting of contemporary Ecole de Paris painting. The strong abstract structures or eddying marks in Milne's best drawing recall Soulages and Hartung respectively. An innate gift for drawing underpins Milne's 'oeuvre'; the confident vigour of the graphic work is translated into his reliefs and forms in the round. The latter carry implications of drawing in terms of linear incisions and shallow depressions, etched or carved into polished, patinated or rough textured surfaces. The rectilinear drawings carry overt architectural associations. Corridors, windows, steps or portals are recalled.

In Paris Milne attended drawing classes at the celebrated Academie de la Grande Chaumiére, a long established school in the heart of Montparnasse where both recognised artists and aspiring students used the same model in the life rooms. The sculptors Emmanuel Auricoste and Ossip Zadkine were among the staff though neither appear to have moved Milne. A puritan streak disposed the northerner to the compact sculpture of Maillol, Dobson and Brancusi. Milne's failure to respond, even thematically, to Zadkine's elaborate symbolic and mythic content highlighted the English sculptor's formalist agenda. From an early stage Milne referred simply, yet emotively, to the 'forms' in his work. Sculpture was a contained plastic entity, constructed on its own terms. Symbolic residues or allusion to subject matter were secondary phenomena.

Milne had gone as far as he could in Paris at the time. A long-standing interest in antiquity meant that a first trip to Greece beckoned. What would be the first of many trips to Greece came in September 1952. The discovery of the classical sites where many of the objects that had moved him at the British Museum and the Musée de Louvre originated, proved revelatory. However much he spoke of the dramatic impact of Greek history or of the power of Greek myth, Milne's foremost endeavour, as a rapidly developing artist, was to extract formal and visual - rather than anthropological - lessons from pre-classical and classical architecture and sculpture. Ancient Greece excelled in many other art forms - ceramics, jewellery and vase painting among them - but it was the physical impact of vast three-dimensional shapes that most affected him. The artist made reference in his notes to the 'massive strength' [4] of mountains encountered near Delphi; he also expressed pleasure for the 'abstract shapes' of architecture, notably long ramps, Doric pillars and monumental propylaea, or gateways, at sites like Delphi, Corinth and the Acropolis.

The 'strong bold forms' of archaic carving proved another vital influence.

In contrast to the inert frontality and frozen symmetry of archaic figures, individual sculptures like the Delphic bronze Charioteer and the marble Calf Bearer from the Athenean Acropolis, both of which were life size, seemed to capture naturalism. These well known sculptures exerted their spell on Milne less for early classical naturalism than for what he described as their 'numbing presence' and 'timelessness of expression'. He also liked the streamlined features of the Charioteer, in particular the long robe, the 'positive stance' of naked feet and the 'elegant gesture' of the outstretched arm. In the later upright polished bronzes Milne seems to simulate such themes. Whatever the case these later bronzes, eponymously linked to Greek, Persian and other ancient cultures, provided further evidence of a fundamental link between the abstract forms of his modernist project and cultural source material based in the distant past.

Throughout the time spent in Paris and Greece Milne responded to the various stimuli graphically. Sculpture would follow later. He needed to master new technical means with which to realise a maturing artistic vision. Late in 1952, returning from his educative travels, Milne trod the well-worn path to St. Ives, Cornwall. Here he entered Hepworth's studio as an unpaid apprentice. By virtue of a rapid assimilation of techniques learnt from Hepworth and her assistant Denis Mitchell, he graduated to being a paid employee at Trewyn. Hepworth detected Milne's graphic abilities, telling him 'when your sculpture is as good as your drawing you will have arrived'. Milne did not in fact arrive as a sculptor until his relatively short spell at Trewyn Studios had ended, though the curvacious, upright carving in guarea, *Vertical Form* (1954) is as strong an example as any that he produced in wood or stone. The other assistants, Mitchell, Leonard, Roger Leigh and Brian Wall among them, stayed with Hepworth for longer. One of them, Brian Wall, later recalled Milne being 'intimidated on one level' [5] by Hepworth, a factor that partly explains his early remove from her immediate influence.

The brevity of his period at Trewyn did not prevent Milne receiving a revealing insight into the life and career of an internationally significant artist at a crossroads. Having consolidated a vast reputation after successful participation at the Venice Biennale in 1950 and at the Festival of Britain the following year, Hepworth embarked on an unprecedented phase of intense work. The carvings led, in 1956, to the issue of the first bronzes and sculptures in sheet metal. Hepworth turned fifty

Top: John Milne. *Cylindrical Form*. 1966.

Bottom left: Liam Hanley. 'Ship and Sculptural Form'.

Bottom right: Michael Canney. *Untitled*. 1984.

John Milne *Vertical Form* (1954). Guarea.

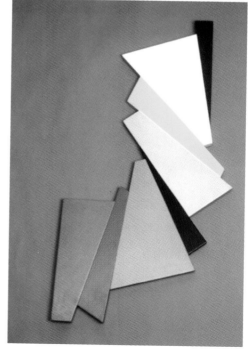

during Milne's first year, and if current preoccupations did not amount to a mid-life crisis then certainly such recent events as the dissolving of her marriage to Ben Nicholson and the death in a plane crash of her son, Paul Skeaping, compelled her to dig deep into inner resources. Her visit to Greece in 1954 was for personal as much as professional reasons and it is tempting to speculate that Milne's earlier experience of Hellenistic culture may have exerted an influence on Hepworth's visit. Like him she spoke of the 'rhythmic' grandeur of the landscape there.

The critic A.M. Hammacher perceived in Hepworth's work up to 1951 'a conception of form which tended to assign to the human figure too important a role in abstract work.' [6] A potential for similar ambiguity between abstract construction and figurative reduction existed in Milne carvings like *Torso*, *The Kiss* and in two 1960 sculptures *Gatos* and *Totemic*. In walnut and Spanish mahogany respectively, *Gatos* and *Totemic* use Brancusi's technique of stacking two or more elements in totem-like arrangements. Milne's Portland stone *The Kiss* differs from Brancusi's limestone and stone prototypes of 1908 in replacing neo-primitive scarifications and other surface details with austere, blank planes, surely a sign of Milne's reductionist, and in particular minimalist, modernity. Equally, the lightly modified mass and bulk of Milne's carvings avoided the complex sequences of holes and other radical intrusions favoured by Hepworth. Milne uses shallow depressions or narrow slits but never opts for Hepworth's fully pierced channels.

As well as eschewing Hepworth's complex dialogue between interior and exterior space, Milne resisted Hepworth's sensual exaggeration of deep space through colour or multi-directional stringing. Hepworth had famously stated that the 'colour in the concavities plunges me into the depth of water, caves, of shadows deeper than the carved concavities themselves'. '7 Milne distanced himself from such sentiments, preferring Brancusi's use of light reflecting surfaces with which to soften the impact of solid, concrete form. The considerable debt owed to Hepworth did not require a wholesale adoption of her style. Milne's interest in sculptural responses to landscape lent his work kinship to the broad landscape-derived abstraction of modern St. Ives painting. He knew and was friendly with many of its leading exponents, painters like Lanyon, Wynter, Wells and Barns-Graham.

Barbara Hepworth. Sculpture in Wood and string.

Milne enjoyed exhibiting his work with such contemporaries in group exhibitions of the Penwith Society of Arts, of which he was an active member from 1956 onwards. This vital institution, founded in 1949 as the official voice of modernist art in Cornwall, also offered prestige and the opportunity to exhibit far beyond Cornwall. In 1961, for example, a Penwith touring exhibition organised by the Arts Council included work by Milne. He was also included in strategically important group surveys like 'Eight British Artists' (which could easily have been labelled 'Eight St. Ives Artists') at a gallery in Washington D.C. in 1959. A two-man show at the Crane Gallery in his native Manchester, shared with his old friend the Stockport-born painter Alan Lowndes, confirmed the relevance of his - and Lowndes's - early Mancunian roots.

Milne was well positioned to profit socially from opportunities in St. Ives. He lived in three different addresses close to the centre of town between arriving in St. Ives in 1952 and finally moving into Trewyn House in 1957. This splendid house, his final domicile, offered unrivalled views across St. Ives Bay, and the secluded grounds allowed the display of large sculptures in a setting as conducive as Hepworth's over the wall. In the next twenty years Milne used this facility to entertain lavishly, running it as an exclusive guesthouse as well as offering sanctuary to kindred spirits. His new-found artistic standing in the town was certainly not harmed by possession of such a facility. He did not, though, enjoy either the social or professional status of Hepworth or the influential painter/critic Patrick Heron, or the local-born painter Peter Lanyon, whose premises at Trewyn Studio, Eagles Nest and Little Park Owles respectively offered similarly salubrious contexts in which to entertain useful guests.

By the end of the 1950s Milne had reached a stage in his career where consolidation of early achievements led to exciting developments during the next decade. Visits to France during the later 1950s showed he had not lost the travel bug, even though Milne focused his energies on establishing himself in St. Ives. A trip to a volcanic region of southern France inspired a first bronze relief *Les Baux* (1959). The medium of relief, which linked graphic flatness to sculptural extension, henceforth becomes a vital component of Milne's 'oeuvre'. In *Les Baux* a surface of striated wires and square window-like recesses derive from the simplified drawings featuring windows, corridors and facetted architectural features in general.

FOOTNOTES:

1. From the artist's notes. Undated. Courtesy Belgrave Gallery, London.
2. Cosmo Rodewald in conversation with the author. Manchester, April 1999.
3. ibid.
4. Artist's notes.
5. Brian Wall in telephone conversation with the author. May 1999.
6. A.M. Hammacher. 'Barbara Hepworth'. p. Thames and Hudson, 1968.
7. See Hammacher, p.90.

4

A Modulated Monumentality

The consistently high standards Milne set himself in the studio contrasted with a quantitively erratic output of work during the 1960s. The artist's inventory of sculpture records nothing during 1961 and 1962; the next four years saw the production of a mere seven pieces. The years 1967 to 1969, on the other hand, were marked by a veritable burst of creative activity, twelve new sculptures appearing in 1967, seventeen in both 1968 and in 1969. True, several of the forty-seven sculptures of the late 1960s are the same sculpture either in original plaster form or editioned in different metals and finishes (polished or patinated bronze and cast or cold cast aluminium). But the evidence of the late 1960s is of an artist in full flow, confident of his abilities, patenting interesting new shapes rich in individuality and adherence to a particular set of exotic or anthropomorphic sources.

The unevenness of Milne's output - a situation repeated in the 1970s - may be due to a combination of professional and personal factors. Clearly, financial strictures prevented Milne emulating Hepworth's large scale later bronzes like 'Single Form' (1963) outside the United Nations in New York, 'Four Square' (walk through) 1966, or 'The Family of Man' (1970). But on a smaller scale Milne's cast sculpture succeeds in creating an impression of vitality, variety and originality of conception. Perfectionist by nature, Milne needed time to absorb the varied influences of the countries he visited. Travelling was itself time consuming and precluded sculpture-making though he made some important drawings in his beloved Greece, which he visited regularly throughout the 1960s, and in Persia and Morocco.

Ivaldo Ferrari outside Marjorie Parr's Gallery, St. Ives, early 1970s.

Milne extended the interest for new places into meeting new people; in the domestic arena he enjoyed cooking and entertaining and ran Trewyn as a select guest house. The rigours of running a large house in this capacity undoubtedly impinged on his activity as a sculptor, though by the latter part of the decade he was helped by an Italian friend Ivaldo Ferrari (who later ran the Marjorie Parr Gallery) and Christine Farrington. A darker side to

the convivial and popular socialite may also have played its part in the ups and downs of Milne's career. His depressive temperament underlined a melancholic streak. He suffered from acute insomnia and, according to Cosmo Rodewald, was periodically plagued by doubts concerning the fate of his enterprise as a sculptor. Milne wrote that 'Insomnia is the worst thing in my life,' [1] an accurate assessment of a plight that contributed to his early death.

One of the sculptures owned by Rodewald, the guarea prototype *Gnathos* (1955), which was later produced in a polished bronze edition of three and a patinated bronze edition, proved one of Milne's best known and memorable sculptures. As well as containing qualities discernibly his own, *Gnathos* also speaks eloquently of the implicit inspiration of modern masters like Brancusi and Giacometti. The squarish format of *Gnathos* which, as its title suggests, is inspired by a jaw, presents the viewer with two very different experiences. From its front the sculpture is a slim helmet with a pair of pointed claws almost touching at midpoint; from the side, however, *Gnathos* is an elongated composition with a wide central 'window'. The exaggerated morphological dichotomy between the two angles betrays the unlikely influence of Giacometti, whose work we know Milne admired. The Swiss sculptor's figures are often flat, broad profiles at the side but squeezed and pin-like in front. The pointed primitive features of *Gnathos* are duplicated in later sculptures like *Tòtemic II* (1969). The same claws almost touch like stalagmites and stalactites at the gaping mouth of a cavernous recess. The years that separate the wood version of *Gnathos* from subsequent bronze editions recall the

Trewyn House, St. Ives. John Milne's *Tòtemic II* (1969) is on the lawn.

long periods that elapsed between several Hepworth carvings and their eventual replication in metal. Hepworth's pre-war carvings like 'Discs in Echelon' (1935) and 'Single Form (Eikon)' (1938) or the wartime 'Landscape Sculpture' (1944) did not find reproduction in metal until 1959, 1963 and 1961 respectively.

Milne's direct abstraction from animal or human forms, which are an intermittent feature within an 'oeuvre' more given to landscape or architectural allusions, align his work most closely with that of Brancusi, the father of modern sculpture, whose use of bird, fish or head motifs provide a distinctive precedent for Milne. *Vertical Form* (1963), a featureless upright guarea form notable for subtly planed surfaces and rhythmic wood veins, bears some comparison with Brancusi's marble 'Seal' of 1943. *Maquette for Leda* and *Leda* (1968) continue the dialogue with the great Romanian, who also produced a sculpture titled 'Leda'. Unlike Brancusi, however, Milne's *Leda* fails to integrate representational and abstract aspects in a satisfactory way. Extruding limbs and arched neck create confusion between the compact integrity of abstract sculpture and a trinket-like craft object.

Unlike sculpture of more overt figurative intention, Milne's simplified forms limited themselves to extracting basic visual or plastic principles like posture, weight, substance and orientation from the monolithic representation of the body. The greater proclivity towards landscape or architecture, sometimes conceived as one and the same, surfaced in *Delphi* (1965), his second bronze relief. After 1962, when he made his second and last trip with Rodewald, Milne visited Greece annually, usually in the company of Stanley Sellers, a Birmingham-based architect who later became a potter. The square relief that is a direct response to these trips is compositionally divided between an upper and lower chamber. Patinated throughout, the surface has a mixture of curved and rectangular depressions, a probable reference to ruined sites, earth features or, in the upper part, to hills or passing cloud. Which-ever way we read it

John Milne at Delphi, Greece 1960s. Richard Butt is with the artist.

Delphi is a satisfying work integrating Milne's interest in drawing, texture and both lateral and upright conceptions of form. The figurative symbolism of the early Manchester relief *Minerva* is replaced with the taut graphic and compositional unity that Milne undoubtedly picked up from Ben Nicholson's reliefs.

The possibility of the figure frinctioning as a quasi-architectural totem or monument owed much to even older sources than that of classical Greece. Hepworth spoke of discovering 'the remarkable

John Milne *Easter Island Form* (1966) Bronze resin.

pagan landscape which lies between St. Ives, Penzance and Lands End; a landscape which still has a very deep effect on me, developing all my ideas about the relationship of the human figure in landscape'. She was making specific reference, in this general statement, to the megalithic quoits and standing stone circles strewn across the ancient hills and moors of south-west Cornwall. The grouped forms in Hepworth's later period paid obvious homage to the enduring stone relics of her neolithic forebears. *Easter Island Form* was Milne's answer; appearing as an editioned bronze maquette in 1966, it was later issued on a much larger scale, six feet tall, in both aluminium and bronze editions in 1969. Milne imbued the surface with a dark, rather than polished, finish in order to absorb light and enhance the opaque mystery of timeless effigies. The anthropomorphic grandeur and almost comic animation of giant stones are qualities replicated in Milne's powerful adaptations. He intrudes with the unmistakeable stamp of a modern artist; a lump of material is subject to subtle shifts of plane and surface, a knowing compromise between solidity and surface fluidity, between simple curved planes and surface modelling, and between an ancient symbol and a modernist object.

The shifting surface inflections of *Easter Island Form* contrasted with the smooth machine-like finish of another single upright form of 1966, *Cylindrical Form*, a patinated bronze edition that, like *Easter Island Form*, re-appeared in 1969 in polished bronze and cold cast aluminium editions. *Cylindrical Form* reminds us of implicit geometric structure in nature and confirms Milne's awareness of sculpture as an object true to itself in terms both of material and formal articulation. The cylinder is interrupted by a V-shaped incision, adding to the curved and flat subtleties of surface orientation while imparting the look of a Brancusian fragment.

A repertoire of new shapes informed Milne's sculpture during 1967, a busy year that witnessed a marked increase in production. The acquisition of new technical means, allowing fibreglass and cold cast bronze and aluminium variations, and the continued inspiration of discovering new places - he made a first trip to Morocco that year - spurred an ostensible departure from previous work. The immediate impact of Morocco did not, however, make any obvious morphological effect on the sculpture until the early 1970s. But new landscape experiences, which triggered sculptural reactions, yielded *Landscape Form* (1967), a patinated bronze whose lively surfaces of flat and curved inflections, including a large central hollow, or valley, flanked by ridges, confirmed the importance of landscape to a sculptor by now hilly enmeshed in the landscape-derived ethos of the abstract St. Ives 'school'. A large 1963 drawing *Zakynthos* had shared with the work of St. Ives painters like Lanyon, O'Malley or Hilton the interpretation of landscape in terms of the figure. Milne wrote of *Landscape Form* as belonging to a strand of work, fulfilled during the following decade, in which the specific landscape effects of 'light, simplicity, above all, space' '2 were translated into the single forms of sculpture. *Landscape Form II* (1967) varied from the first, larger, sculpture in containing a prominent conic feature, an obvious allusion to a mountain.

Subsequent visits to Morocco, during the spring and autumn of both 1968 and 1969, became a regular occurrence during the first half of the 1970s. But Greece also continued to exert its hold and distinctive new sculptures, *Anakalypsis* (1967) and *Deimos* (1968) bore Greek titles. Both sculptures were cast in bronze editions, *Deimos* polished, *Anakalypsis* patinated, and each was followed by a much larger, this time unique, version in cold cast bronze. The chunky stacked form of *Deimos* continued the Brancusian idea of two forms in

John Milne
Anakalypsis (1967)
Bronze resin.

one; the lower part resolutely earth-bound, the upper section disposed to evoke the idea of ascension. The squat, primitive solemnity notwithstanding, *Deimos* anticipated a series of related works - *Icarus* (1967), *October Form* (1970), *Phobus* (1971) and *Syrinx* (1976) among them - that continued to exploit dynamic shifts between gravity and ascension.

The smoothed surface of *Deimos* contrasted with the pitted, patinated surface texture of both the unique large scale and the small editioned maquette of *Anakalypsis*. These textures impart the character of weathered objects, a reading validated by a sharply rising parabolic curve that resembles a breaking wave. *Anakalypsis* is certainly akin to Hepworth's sculptures with avowed maritime associations. In her earliest St. Ives carvings, like 'Wave' (1944) and 'Pelagos' (1946), Hepworth specifically referred the pure spatial language of constructivist form to natural phenomena like opening buds, spiralling waves and sea movements in general. She subsequently pursued these associations, both through textural and morphological means, in bronzes like 'Curved Form (Trevalgan)' (1956), 'Corymb' (1959) and in a sheet metal composition 'Stringed Figure (Curlew)' (1956). Constructing form with sheet metal enabled Hepworth to model around versatile and malleable sheets - usually expanded aluminium - investing a new subtlety to the range of attainable shapes. *Anakalypsis* also benefits from the structural possibilities provided by sheet metal armatures.

The similarity between *Anakalypsis* and the Hepworth pieces in question begs consideration of the general relationship between the two artists who, after Milne moved into Trewyn House at the end of 1956, were neighbours. The property, once part of a larger estate comprising both Milne's house and Hepworth's Studios, had been purchased in 1956 by Cosmo Rodewald from a Mrs. Goodhand. The original estate had been owned by a Cornish family, the Trewellas, who partitioned the whole and sold the lower part to Hepworth in 1949 and the top part - which was later bought for Milne - to Goodhand. Brian Wall amusingly recalled that Milne 'liked the idea that he lived above her,' [3] his instalment in the grander half of the original estate smoothly accommodating the reality of Hepworth's greater professional status in the art world at large.

Milne was nearly thirty years Hepworth's junior and their relationship cordial and friendly though mediated by a formal professional distance - had no competitive edge. Milne maintained, throughout his life, considerable fondness and respect for Hepworth who in turn encouraged her former assistant. Encouragement sometimes turned to practical help. On several occasions she countered Milne's restlessness by urging him to stay in St. Ives and concentrate on work. As early as 1959 she detected Milne's angst and advised that 'you should only work at this moment and delay decisions.' [4] Later that year she paid him the compliment of confirming the value of his presence as a neighbour, confiding to him that 'quiet privacy means so much to me for my work that the mere thought of what might happen if you moved gives me acute anxiety.' [5]

During 1965 Milne sold the bottom of his garden to Hepworth, who needed more space. The money from the transaction enabled Milne to build a garden studio away from the not infrequent social distractions of the main house. Hepworth occasionally visited Milne, when a casual glance at recent work led to encouraging words. She took a fuller glance at Milne's work one Saturday afternoon in early April 1972 when, in London for her exhibition at the Marlborough Gallery, she visited the younger man's solo exhibition at the Marjorie Parr Gallery. According to Milne's friend Brian Smith, Hepworth's secretary between 1968 and 1975 - who accompanied Hepworth on the visit to Kings Road to see Milne's show - Hepworth was 'reluctant to give opinions about other artists' work.' [6] Clearly her influential position as a public figure and influential artist made it necessary to guard against too close an alignment with other artists' causes. Her particular interest in Milne's work extended to her looking hard at it only when time and responsibilities allowed. Circumstances did not allow her to see Milne's retrospective at Plymouth in 1971 even though he had attended Hepworth's Tate Gallery retrospective in 1968.

Financial strictures precluded Milne emulating the large outdoor scale of many Hepworth sculptures. During the 1950s before bronze casting was the norm for either, wood carving was one affordable way to work on a large scale. But he did not have either Hepworth's virtuoso carving talents or her means to be able to employ assistants to reduce labour demands. Milne's earlier carvings are generally smaller in scale. Hepworth had once encouraged him to tackle scale, however, writing to him in 1959 that 'it would be very good if you carried out some work for out of doors and had it on view in your most perfect setting in your garden.' [7] When he did use enhanced scale, as in the case of *Deimos*, *Totemic II* and *Easter Island Form* (1969), each of which stands approximately six foot, Milne had to budget for casting them by the cheaper cold cast method. By the late 1960s Milne had established the physical and conceptual parameters of his sculpture and was used to working in scale from small maquettes for a glass cabinet or mantelpiece to free-standing forms roughly conforming to human height. At this point in his development he had opted for a kind of 'small is beautiful' ethos, resistant to rhetorical or grandiloquent gesture and to gratuitous scale. Joining Hepworth for drinks one warm June evening in 1968 he was greatly impressed by a relatively modest size sculpture, inspired by the Isles of Scilly, called 'Six Forms (2x3)', from a selection of outdoor pieces placed in the grounds. It is still there, positioned in what is now the Barbara Hepworth Museum. Milne felt at ease with his own language and the criterion of size was largely irrelevant to either the sculptural integrity or the expressive powers of his work. In Milne's Plymouth retrospective catalogue Bryan Robertson would be justified in writing that there was 'no difference in intensity between the very large or small works, or relaxation of tension.' [8]

The sequential development of Milne's sculpture often yielded novelty from formal backtracking; fragments or combinations of fragments from previous works are often responsible for the new 'look' of many pieces. *Vertical Form*, cast in cold cast bronze and aluminium editions, was a more complex paraphrase of the minimal *Cylindrical Form*. It shared with its simpler brethren the same V-shaped notch, a subtle though distinctive feature that contributed to the upward zig zag. Consistent to most of Milne's work, *Vertical Form* has no Hepworthian holes, though a characteristic vertical slit near its base introduces the possibility of a thin interior. The sculpture has dynamic tension between the object as an abstract construction of interlocking cubes and rectangles and, on a thematic level, a schematic pair of embraced figures. This tension between form and content, encouraged by the employment of exotic and evocative titles, never subverted or compromised the integrity of the sculpture as a thing in itself. This factor allowed Robertson the chance to observe that the sculpture was 'often mysterious, but only in origin, never in its concrete sculptural identity'. [9] The perceived formalism was epitomised in another vertical sculpture, *Project* (1969), comprising a tall column shooting up from what the same writer described as a pair of 'rigidly clamping petals' at its base.

The production of reliefs, a prominent feature of his output during the years 1966 to 1968, resurfaced during 1972. Linking the flatness of drawing with raised medallion-like profiles, Milne's reliefs achieve a playful arrangement of line, texture and plane. Architecture is not always the inspiration behind them and however architectonic they sometimes appear are often about elusive moments of natural flux, as in the case of *Wave* (1967) and *Clouds* (1970). The former, an important relief - one of Milne's largest - signifies the heaving weight and rhythmic movement of the sea. *Storm Descending* and *Storm Lifting* (1968) are also inspired by ephemeral natural phenomena and call into play the ability of sculpture to make conceptually bold and imaginative interpretations in concrete formal terms. In fact, like much contemporary St. Ives painting, the 'storm' reliefs interpret subjective landscape experience within the formalised language of abstraction. Both reliefs are essentially sequences of broken rectangular planes, thin vertical channels or raised bars balancing the lateral inclination of the sliced rectangles. Robertson described *Storm Descending* as an ingenious piece of symbolic subterfuge relaying a storm over the south of France; 'an immensely black sky... pushing down to the earth and bounded and offset by a blazing white horizontal band of light along the horizon's rim.' [10] The horizontal and vertical axes Mondrian divined in nature and extracted from landscape provided the cue for Milne. Not alone in making such sculptural interpretations of landscape - Hubert Dalwood did the same in the 'Mirage' series of 1966 as well as in miniature 'tableau' environments during the 1970s - Milne did so in terms that conceived sculpture essentially as a monolithic object or, where the reliefs were concerned, as a kind of extended drawing made concrete.

By 1969 the reliefs were replaced by bulky new sculptures. However, two new pieces - *Horus* and *Trio* - were slim and upright, with a hint of Brancusi's three-in one totemic arrangements. Notch-like forms swell from a central column at base, midriff and apex. Both were polished bronze editions, *Trio* akin to an obsolete utility or ritual object (like Gaudier-Brzeska's doorknocker). *Horus*, the taller of the pair, was described by Robertson as an erect 'formalised reptile'. The residual form of a large recumbent human figure is, however, a redolent feature of *Open Torso* (1969), a cold cast bronze which, like *Prometheus* (1967) reads as a limbless torso or classical figure fragment. The cold cast aluminium sculptures *Flight* and *Turning Form*, the former horizontal the latter vertical in orientation, reveal Milne's continued inventiveness, most particularly in the characteristic shaping of inert, lumpy blocks of

John Milne
Prometheus (1967).
Bronze resin.

material with subtle surface modulation, changes of direction, shallow cavities and curved or angular depressions. They are the inevitable outcome of a collusion between modelling and carving, the two modes that dominated his earlier work and which now operated in an implicit accord.

The ongoing process of shaping lumps of matter in this manner was, during the 1970s, discerned by several critics sympathetic to Milne's work. Bernard Denvir described Milne's 'shifting planes and restrained internal movement,' [11] while the abstract painter Denis Bowen, reviewing the sculptor's next Marjorie Parr exhibition in 1974, witnessed that, irrespective of scale, Milne's pieces 'are charged with a modulated monumentality and strength.' [12]

The 'shifting planes' and 'modulated monumentality' of these sculptures depart considerably from the geometric symmetry of Hepworth and, if anything, possess - albeit in terms of opaque volume - something of Gabo's feeling for continuous spatial interplay and multi-directional movement. A small polished bronze, *Intaglio* (1969), on the other hand, is a simple flat-sided object relying on reflectiveness to tease spatial ambiguity out of closed, inert, boulder-like form. The clean-cut surfaces are complemented with the inscription of three dark grooves, akin to the start of an unfulfilled constructivist symphony of intersecting or diverging lines.

The busy exhibiting schedule of the late 1960s, which culminated in his large Plymouth retrospective in June 1971, saw a mixture of group and solo displays. During the first half of the decade Milne contented himself with contributions to the AIA Gallery in London and the Penwith Gallery, St. Ives. During the winter of 1967/68 he exhibited in 'Six West Country Sculptors', a touring exhibition organised by Plymouth City Art Gallery, which was a prelude to his solo show there. Milne's status as an established west country sculptor saw his work displayed in the open air at Widcombe Manor, Bath, a large property owned by Jeremy Fry, an inventor and heir to the Fry chocolate fortune. Fry was well-connected with local sculptors like Lynn Chadwick. Milne's sculpture also complemented contemporary Cornish painting. He contributed to a group exhibition of St. Ives artists at the Austin Reed Gallery and Travers Gallery, both in London, and also showed as one of six St. Ives artists in October 1968 at the Peterloo Gallery in Manchester. Here Milne was the only sculptor among a group who included Bryan Wynter, Michael Snow and Brian Illsley. During the following summer Milne displayed with sculptors, among them Hepworth and Denis Mitchell, at the Sheviock Gallery, Torpoint. The decade was seen out with a solo exhibition of sculpture (with Breon O'Casey paintings) at the Marjorie Parr Gallery, London, where, throughout these important years of professional consolidation, he would establish a commercial and critical reputation.

That critical reputation won Milne plaudits from influential quarters, Bryan Robertson at once promoting Milne as an original whose work was neither part of the St. Ives school nor part of fashionable sixties sculpture at large. As a director of the Whitechapel Art Gallery, London, Robertson played a leading role in promoting 'New Generation' sculpture, distinctive features of which - use of synthetic materials, bright eye-catching colour and open minimal or geometric structures - were notably absent from Milne's work. Several sixties sculptors, Dalwood, William Turnbull and Michael Kenny among them, related their reduced forms back to antique or primitive sources. Milne followed suit and thereby joined a quiet anthropomorphic strain of 60's sculpture. In the 1969 Parr exhibition Robertson saw many 'predatory' and 'hieratic' forms, and detected throughout 'an invented anatomy', [13] a feature that underlined Milne's skilful arrangements of abstract form to accommodate elements of figurative content.

FOOTNOTES:

1. John Milne. Private undated notes from the artist's archive.
2. ibid.
3. Brian Wall in conversation with the author, May 1999.
4. Barbara Hepworth letter to John Milne. 15/2/59. Courtesy Brian Smith, St. Ives.
5. Hepworth to Milne. 31/12/59. Courtesy Brian Smith.
6. Brian Smith in conversation with the author, St. Ives, May 1999.
7. Barbara Hepworth letter to John Milne. 15/2/59.
8. Bryan Robertson. Catalogue Introduction for John Milne retrospective, Plymouth, June 4-July 11, 1971.
9. ibid.
10. Bryan Robertson. Review of Marjorie Parr exhibition, 'The Spectator', 18/10/69.
11. Bernard Denvir. 'London Letter'. 'Art International' Vol. 16/5. 20/5/72.
12. Denis Bowen. 'Arts Review'. Oct. 1974.
13. Bryan Robertson. 'Studio International'. Oct. 1969.

5

The 1970s: A Plastic Austerity

During the 1970s Milne's output of sculpture outstripped that of his entire previous 'oeuvre'. It could be argued that Milne responded to the 'zeitgeist' of the new decade by introducing a new productive urgency into his work. Technical standards were raised and the experimental frenzy and youthful speculation that characterised the 'sixties' as a whole gave way to a greater hard-headedness. Milne had always made durable and collectable objects and was professionally, not to say temperamentally, removed from the wayward dematerialised art 'forms' of certain strains of contemporary avant-garde sculpture. The employment of able technical assistants like Tommy Rowe, Colin Hadley and Dirk Rayner enabled Milne to meet deadlines and fulfil the growing demands of exhibition schedules.

John Milne (right) on Porthmeor Beach with *Wave Form* (1972). With him are Tommy Rowe and Colin Hadley.

The most demanding event of this period proved also the most significant of his entire exhibiting career - the retrospective at Plymouth City Art Gallery in June 1971. It consolidated his achievement to date and proved the tonic that spurred a burst of late sculpture during the seven remaining years of his career. The large well-lit room into which a full range of Milne's work was crammed - encompassing small maquettes in glass cabinets, large monolithic or multi-part sculpture, wall-bound reliefs in various metals and small, medium and large scale works on paper - presented an impression of diversity built on thematic unity. Prominently-displayed sculptures like *Anakalypsis*, *Gnathos*, *Leda*, *Deimos*, *Landscape Form* and the recent six-part *Variations* (1971), repeated a number of shapes in different orientations or combinations. A residual anthropomorphic feeling, akin to, but not literally descriptive of, totems, primitive stone arrangements or ancient objects dredged from the seabed, countered the streamlined abstraction that, as it became more prominent in his subsequent sculpture, helped place his later works in a late modernist orbit of minimalism.

Old anxieties and torments returned to haunt him throughout this period, however, and he sought escape through travel as frequently as in previous years. The discovery of Persia, together with more regular visits to Morocco, inspired him and made a mark on the sculptures, some of which bear titles based on these exotic and ancient places. Certainly the challenge of the Plymouth exhibition triggered more agonising, in particular how best to spend available funds. Should he re-cast *Landscape Form*, do a larger cast of *Poseidon*, or make editions of new forms for the show? Also in his notes are laments over the missed architectural opportunities of Plymouth's bland post-war reconstructed city centre. These show he thought seriously about architecture and about sculpture's position in relation to the man-made environment. The disillusion of these notes contrasts with the excitement and wonder that form the tone of his private remarks about Persian cities and Moroccan landscape vistas. Visiting Plymouth to prepare for his retrospective, he dismissed the 'concrete wilderness' [1] before his eyes as evidence of an 'unbelievable lack of imagination on the part of the architects responsible for this grotesque parody of England in 'the thirties'. [2] Hepworth's pre-war collaboration with architects like Gropius, Wells Coates and Leslie Martin formed a precedent for quintessential design standards that could not fail to rub off on any of the young sculptors, like Milne, who were fortunate enough to work in her orbit in post-war St. Ives. Milne's penchant for good design, discernable not only in art but in his choice of interior decor and arrangements of large gardens, reflected these standards.

The success of the retrospective was a source of great relief. More success followed close on the heels of this exhibition. He won the sculpture prize in Westward Television's open art exhibition. In September 1971 the Tate Gallery acquired its first Milne piece, the well-known *Gnathos*, an event no doubt prompted by a Board of Trustees among whom still sat Barbara Hepworth. The following spring Milne enjoyed a second one-man show with Marjorie Parr in London, a large exhibition of thirty-six sculptures in the round - or in the pyramid and cube - and ten reliefs. This bountiful exhibition, staged less than a year after Plymouth, presented a plethora of recent sculpture, all produced since the previous year's retrospective. It showed that, far from resting on laurels, Milne had been galvanised into life, producing a spate of new forms that were significant for the way they showed the recent impact of Turkey, Persia and Morocco. A trip to Turkey had been made immediately after the Plymouth show and a cold cast bronze relief *Ephesus* (1972), displayed in the Parr show, was inspired by one of the ancient sites he visited. Other reliefs shown at Parr included the seminal *Les Baux* and the white fibreglass *Icarus*, a cast of which was owned by the film-maker John Schlesinger.

According to the critic Bernard Denvir, the importance of new Milne sculptures like *Persian Monolith*, *Zagora II*, *Landscape Isfahan*, *Sahara Forms*, or *Atlas* was that they introduced broader references and 'an allusive quality', [3] thereby countering what Denvir saw as the generic 'insularity' of Cornish art. He also detected a 'plastic austerity... beyond the romantic naturalism' of many Hepworth pieces. What was by now clear was that Milne had become both an established St. Ives artist (at a time when the avant garde significance of St. Ives was on the wane) and a restless, cosmopolitan-minded spirit unsure of whether his future lay in an isolated and, in the geographical sense at least, peripheral part of the British Isles. The increased studio production hid the insecurity and relentless soul-searching of his later years.

The lifestyle pertaining throughout Milne's St. Ives years - work stints and domestic responsibilities alleviated by two or three foreign trips each year - remained the pattern to the end. The balance between work and play seemed ideal but proved disruptive to a quiet routine; crucially, the escalating costs of maintaining his lifestyle brought new financial pressures that the increased production of sculpture alone could not remedy. The oil crisis of 1973/4 triggered global inflation which increased the cost of living overnight. Brian Smith recalled that, despite Milne's 'tremendous driving force' [4] as an artist he was 'always seeking to escape responsibilities' and, more particularly, 'the gloom and darkness of English winters', for which he seemed to have developed a phobia. 'He only relaxed in the sun', Smith concluded. Milne enjoyed an opulent and lavish lifestyle. Stanley Sellers's description of a 'glossy' lifestyle saw the use of top hotels and restaurants in Venice, Athens, London and other locations. Milne contemplated leaving St. Ives altogether. He looked at properties in Surrey and near Lewes in Sussex, where Cosmo Rodewald owned a second home. Nothing came of these initiatives though it may have only been his untimely death that prevented a remove from Cornwall in the 1980s or after.

Travels during the 1970s fuelled many ideas for sculpture. In 1971 he wrote that Persia had 'as great an impact upon my work as those early visits to Greece and Morocco'. [5] The titles of many 1971/72 sculptures bear witness to the inspiration of the Near East. *Shiraz* and *Persepolis* (1971) were followed, in 1972, by *Cyrus*, *Persian Monolith*, *Landscape (Isfahan)*, *Darius* and a relief *Shah Abbas*. The small scale of *Shiraz*, *Cyrus* and *Darius* did not diminish the evocation of ancient burial chambers, intricate urban spaces and secular Persian architecture in general. In Isfahan Milne recounted seeing the 'the most staggeringly beautiful architecture' he had ever encountered. *Landscape (Isfahan)* was Milne's response, though the piece is less a monument than a landscape-evoking tableau, one that sets out a

John Milne *Persepolis* (1971) Bronze.

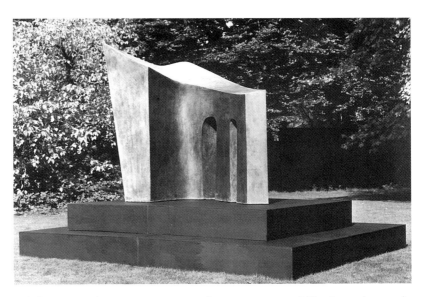

miniature environment separate from our own. Milne's sculpture is less theatrical or metaphorical than that of another sculptor, Hubert Dalwood, who made tableaux and reliefs in response to the inspiration of ancient buildings and spaces. A pair of pyramids in the Milne piece have as much formal as symbolic significance.

The extended base of *Landscape (Isfahan)* was repeated in other pieces which use space, interval and rhythm to refer to the openness of Moroccan landscape. The sliced segments and truncated rhythms of the wafer-thin stainless steel *Desert Forms* (1972) are also set on an extended base, albeit one that is no longer part of the sculptural syntax. The base reverts to a more conventional role, supporting the sculpture from which it is differentiated through its separate material. The base nonetheless offers a ground-like plane from which topographically elevated forms impart a model-like replication of a real landscape. *Sahara Form II* (1971), by virtue of a straight or grooved incline, also seems to turn the sculpture, now a solid, polished bronze object, into a miniature landscape environment, one that associates with the distinct waves and undulations of desert or mountain chain.

Milne also used the texture of wood to make landscape associations. Within a tight corner of formal abstraction, Milne made ingenious structures that captured the perceptual echoes of the north African landscape. *Horizontal Form (Sahara)* (1971), a streamlined, gently inclined mahogany, uses the broad graining to evoke sand. A much more intricate carving in walnut, *Atlas* (1972), does the same, though the serrated edges and notches focus on the grand landscape plan. The carving led to a bronze edition, *Atlas II* (1974), where the exploitation of, and interplay between, opaque patinated and reflective polished surfaces assumed almost mimetic and parodic proportions. The artist described 'two long forms in echelon, the outer sides patinated, the insides burnished to a golden finish... carved in a jagged formation which reflects in the polished inner surface of the opposite one; as the mountain ridges in the blazing sun'. [6] Milne was captivated by gorges, which he described as 'terrifying yet eternal', and a later sculpture, *Draa* (1974) took its name from a long meandering Moroccan valley.

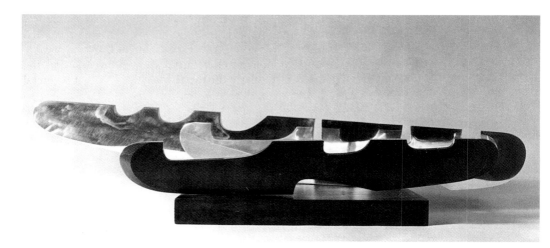

Milne summarised Morocco as 'predominantly the land of the desert, the sun and mountains.' The importance of the sun inspired several sculptures which use the complete geometric symbol of the circle as a starting point for an imaginative manipulation of inert materials to convey energy, flux, warmth, reflection and other attributes we might associate with the sun. Hepworth also invested the concrete language of sculpture with symbolic overlay. In her 1969 'Disc and Strings (Sun)', a bent, pierced and stringed circle of sheet metal aligns its geometric symmetry with fleeting solar phenomena like sunrays. Like much of his sculpture, *Aten* (1972), a large circular polished bronze with a patinated core, reads like a free-standing relief. The form has a pronounced front and back, but little of strategic interest at the sides. The sculpture does, though have an interior, a shallow patinated recess exemplifying Bryan Robertson's description of a generic 'elusive density'. [7] *Helios* (1972), another polished bronze, uses as its title the Greek word for sun (Aten derives from an Egyptian word meaning 'sun god'), which it evokes, not through a disc but through the golden, polished finish of the boat-shaped surface. *Helios* has morphological kinship to the carving *Horizontal Form (Sahara)*, and to bronzes like *Sahara Form II* or *Draa*, an indication that Milne's sculpture cross-fertilised, combined or recycled ideas throughout this period. *Hera* (1972), a slightly larger, upright polished bronze, repeated the flat formalised arrangements of kindred 1972 bronzes but has a totemic power based on three truncated circles, a format that, as well as positing possible solar associations (like the sun's movement across the sky) derives from two stainless steel constructions, *Three Circles* and *Squares and Circles* (1972), which Milne made during this highly productive year.

The stainless steel sculptures, which recall Hepworth's 'Square Forms' (1962) or the Rietveld Pavilion bronze 'Squares with Two Circles' (1963), offer rare examples of Milne working in a direct constructional mode. Unlike Hepworth and a younger sculptor, Robert Adams (1917-84) - who spent time in St. Ives during the 1950s and again in the mid 1970s (when he acted as head of sculpture at Falmouth School of Art) - Milne did not solder or weld metal. Adams' later bronzes, which were exhibited alongside those of Milne at the Marjorie Parr Gallery, were often cast from wood maquettes, confirming Adams' roots as a worker in wood, which he either carved or constructed. Although carved sculpture, using a refreshing variety of wood, remained an intermittent feature of Milne's 'oeuvre' the bulk of his sculpture, particularly during the 1970s, was cast in metal (usually bronze) from carefully prepared plasters. Bryan Robertson wrote in 1971 that much of Milne's work was 'arrived at by modelling, as much as by carving', [8] and it is certainly true that the later bronzes owed their balance, poise and refinement to originating plasters that were modelled in initial stages and then subjected to the precision finish that carving, filing or other erasing processes allowed.

The convergence of figurative, landscape and architectural ideas in Milne's abstract sculpture reflected his admiration for the principles of figurative proportion in classical architecture. The integration of architecture with the landscape also intrigued him. During 1973, a quiet year sandwiched between the two most productive years of his career, he travelled twice to Morocco, in the spring and autumn. Perhaps because of this only three sculptures appeared in 1973, of

which *Prometheus* and *Persepolis II*, were large scale cold cast bronze versions of pieces originally made in 1967 and 1971 respectively. The one entirely new form, *Oneiros*, was one of the most intriguing to emerge to date. The following year J.P. Hodin wrote that *Oneiros*, the Greek for 'dream figure', functioned as 'a monument to Hypnos, the Greek God of Sleep'. [9] The sculpture has an in-built mysteriousness relaying the random thought waves of sleep in terms of fluctuating surface patterns and unexpected features.

In common with much late sculpture, *Oneiros* is a formal composite paraphrasing features from previous work. *Oneiros* uses the claws of *Gnathos* and *Totemic*, which extend like pointed limbs from the main trunk or column. Discernible in Milne's exhibition of mainly 1974 sculpture at the Marjorie Parr Gallery during October of that year was a tendency for sculpture to pair off into morphological sequences. By this stage bronze was the favoured material; economic factors decreed that larger items, such as *Megalith II*, *Propylaea II*, and *Horizontal Form II* were replicated in the cheaper

John Milne *Oneiros* (1973). Bronze resin.

material of cold cast bronze. Nevertheless, two thirds of the thirty sculptures displayed at Parr's gallery were bronze (all seven reliefs were cold cast bronze), a factor confirming Milne's level of investment in the enterprise. Allusion to landscape or maritime themes dominated the 1974 output; a return to figurative themes, which would characterise the last three years' work, was only apparent in *Athena* and *Oneiros*; an apt pairing of sentinel-like forms. Milne wrote that 'both appear to be watching or surveying.' [10] Small forms like *Waves* and *Sea Form* prompted Hodin, author of the catalogue, to describe 'stylised transcriptions of fluidity into solid shapes.' [11]

From the fluidity of water to the monumental uprightness of *Athena* and *Oneiros* and on to the expansive landscape conception of *Todra* and *Landscape (Isfahan)*, the sculptures at Parr presented a diversity of sculptural responses. The sliced channels of *Atlas* and *Lemenja* , *Corinthos* and *Chrysalis* (1974), later repeated in *Wave Turning* (1976), became a stylistic signature tune, a by-product of Milne's landscape experiences in Greek or Moroccan gorges and narrow valleys.

John Milne *Todra* (1974). Bronze.

Both Hodin's catalogue essay and Michael Goedhuis's sympathetic review in 'Studio International' indicated Milne's success in laying aside the ghost of Hepworth and establishing an independent voice. The 'Herald Tribune (New York)' noted that 'his voice is uniquely his own.' [12] Hodin saw the influence of Hepworth on Milne as positive and salutary, a generic factor enabling one receptive artist to develop from, and build on, the achievements of another. Goedhuis's preference was for *Credo* (1974), an upright fork-like form in polished bronze which 'succeeds better than most' in its avoidance of 'literal allusions to antique subject-matter or location.' [13] Anticipating the raised 'arms' of *Resurgence* (1976) and *Supplication* (1978), *Credo* stands, three foot in height, as an elegant, if slightly leaning, asymmetric form. Its austere, pared-down surfaces, pure yet a little awkward and unpredictable, perhaps represent a puritanical streak in Milne's northern sensibility. Illustrated on the Parr catalogue cover, *Credo* was obviously something of a centrepiece for the exhibition. It also exemplified what Denis Bowen described as 'those principles, so associated with St. Ives, where precision of craftsmanship and simplicity of form are structurally compounded.' [14] Milne bore this out, writing in 1978 that *Credo* (together with *Resurgence* and other late pieces) reached a minimal-like synthesis between conception and process, one where 'nothing more could be added to, or taken away from' *15 the final image.

The success of the Parr exhibition owed much to Allan Dunn who, along with Tommy Rowe, proved an invaluable source of help in preparing the rough bronze casts after their return from either the Art Bronze Foundry in Chelsea or the Morris Singer in Basingstoke, Hampshire. Rowe represented a link between Milne, Hepworth and Denis Mitchell, the versatile Cornish-born craftsman helping out in the studios of all three. But whereas he carved in Hepworth's studio and confessed to a closer involvement with Mitchell - whom he had known since the age of 15 - Rowe worked alone in Milne's studio. Here strenuous and painstaking grinding and filing rough casts were followed by polishing, patinating and, finally, mounting the sculptures on smart marble, slate or wood bases. According to Rowe, Milne 'didn't do a lot in the studio,' *16 electing to make drawings in the main house and leaving the laborious preparations to his part-time assistant at the bottom of the garden.

While never equalling that of 1972 and 1974, the output of the last four years yielded several interesting new forms, some unprecedented others amounting to formal rearrangements of previous shapes. *Birdsong* (1975), *Contrapuntal Forms* and *Maenads* (1976), for example, looked like entirely new departures. *Birdsong* Milne saw as offering a hopeful message at a time when, increasingly tormented by chronic insomnia, he looked coldly at his work in the middle of the night and concluded that 'the total impression is of conflict.' *17 The patinated lower forms of *Birdsong*, suggestive of a nest or enveloping cocoon, tapered into a slim bird-like apex. Recalling Brancusi's 'Maistra', Milne substitutes Brancusi's diversity of stacked materials for a unified monument in which variety is the product of changing surface texture. In a creative play of finish Milne exchanges verdigris at base for a high reflective polish at the top. The surface variety gave the sculpture a symbolic veneer, one to do with the ascent from the darkness of earth to the light of the sky.

The notes that Milne wrote at night impart a troubled mood. A 'more troubled or questioning phase' *18 was Milne's explanation for *Contrapuntal Forms*, an elegantly poised composition, however, that showed no relaxation of energy and imagination. Despite sharing its title with one of Hepworth's best known sculptures (shown in 1951 at the Festival of Britain) *Contrapuntal Forms* compresses two main figure-like forms into a close alignment, one where the monumental integrity of the object - originating in a single material or overall form - is intact. The tension between two forms in one recalls not Hepworth, but Brancusi, whose own use of this device was a seminal influence on Milne's early adaptation of 'The Kiss'. Several of Hepworth's late works, by contrast, used horizontal dispersal or multiplicity of elements across a large base.

A number of new sculptures, which derive titles from Greek or Egyptian myth, once again draw on figurative sources. Not for the first time Milne's work operated in tandem between two or more dominant themes. The late work, dominated by the medium of polished bronze, unexpectedly threw up three new carved sculptures, in guarea. They are *Returning Form* (1976), *Vertical Form* (1977) and

Group (1978). Similarly, sculptures with figurative resonance were accompanied by new sculptures which the artist described as possessing an 'architectural feel'. '[19] The latter, taking their cue from the uncompromisingly geometric *Divided Cone* (1974), led to several late sculptures like *Obelisk* (1974), *Cheops* and *Duet*, each of which celebrate the simple constructional principles of architecture. A disarming simplicity attends sculptures which use archtypal cube, cylinder or pyramid shapes. Like a standardised Judd or Morris cube, these works rely on a uniform, not varied finish; their almost unmodulated surface 'colour' - reflective polished bronze - allows light a role in the complication and distortion of concrete forms. Such works sit with a fresh authority. *Nyktos* (1974) actually inhabits the ground plane, without the mediating support of a plinth, and in so doing interacts with the spectator - and the surrounding environment - in a more direct way. The minimal-like reduction of these later works are the product of an attained maturity, where the artist has worked through his influences and inspirations to reach an expression of contained power.

The final phase of Milne's career witnessed a busy exhibiting schedule, ranging from perfunctory group exhibitions in Cornwall - principally at the Penwith and Wills Lane galleries in St. Ives and the Orion Gallery in Newlyn - to prestigious and challenging venues much further afield. A mixed exhibition at the Allan Edwardes Gallery, Vancouver in 1974 was a prelude to several solo and group shows in North America. An exhibition in January 1976, shared with Denis Mitchell and Enzo Plazzotta in Saudi Arabia, was followed, during May, by a group exhibition at the Genesis Galleries in New York City. A year later he exhibited here again, in a survey 'The Best of British Art'. During 1977 Milne had several solo exhibitions - in May at the Lad Lane Gallery, Dublin; in June at Saltram House, Plymouth; in October at the Ben Mangel Gallery, Philadelphia; and finally at the Allen House Gallery, Louisville, Kentucky at the end of the eventful year. The National Trust grounds at Saltram, Plymouth proved an ideal setting for large outdoor pieces like *Persepolis*. The 'Western Morning News' reported that many of the 34 sculptures on display 'bear witness to the influence of the ancient architecture and mythology' '[20] of Greece, North Africa and the Near Fast. The frequency of exhibitions confirmed the growing reputation Milne was enjoying during the last two years, a factor that underlines the professional, as well as personal, tragedy of his untimely demise.

The titles allocated to many sculptures produced during these last two years of his career did indeed betray a common theme in ancient myth. Perhaps more significantly the sculptures share striking formal correspondences. *Maenads* and *Contrapuntal Forms; Thor* (1974) and *Sentinel* (1976); *Osiris, Anubis* (1977) and *Isis* (1976); *Duo* and *Supplication* (1978) are kindred brethren within a coherent repertoire of shapes that discretely integrate form and content. Isis and Osiris were husband and wife in Egyptian myth and in the two sculptures Milne produced after them he squeezes subtle morphological variation - mainly between concave and convex nuances - out of a pair of conjugal forms. Both pieces stand like figures. The stance of *Anubis* is also insistently figurative, albeit in the stylised terms of an abstracted monument. A pair of 1976 forms, *Bacchae* and *Pavan*, again suggest the figure, the former investing the academic prototype of a limbless torso with a mysterious biomorphic energy. Bacchae and Maenads were, in fact, mythological women who celebrated the power of Dionysus in terms of dance and music. Within the tight aesthetic terms of largely non-narrative and non-descriptive abstracted sculpture, Milne alludes to the theme of movement and dance through the plastic device of fluctuating surfaces. The final polished bronzes create looking glass distortions, and with them impressions of fleeting movement.

The publication of a book on Milne's work in 1977 consolidated the sculptor's reputation in the penultimate year of his life. Written by J.P. Hodin, a long-standing friend of, and an author on, Barbara Hepworth, the book illustrates all phases of Milne's career. In particular, an illustration of sculpture strewn across the lawn of Milne's home proved that he had followed Hepworth's advice in 1959 and 'carried out some work for out of doors.' A growing feeling of loneliness and isolation, however, seemed to point to professional frustrations. Cornwall felt a long way from Marjorie Parr and the London art market. The time spent travelling may have been put to better professional use had he taught in art schools. Teaching may have diverted attention from his personal problems. Perhaps partly because he was not London-based and not an art school visitor, Milne was not represented in key surveys of contemporary British sculpture. The Tate Gallery's 'Sculpture of the Sixties', in 1965, the ICA's 'British Sculpture out of the Sixties in 1970 and the Royal Academy's 'British Sculptors 72' of 1972 failed to include Milne, a symptom of the fact of St. Ives's eclipse as an avant garde centre. But twenty years after his death, art fashion has turned full circle and embraced St. Ives' achievement. The chief agent in institutionalising this achievement has been the Tate Gallery, St Ives. For much of the period since it opened in 1993, this popular regional branch of the Tate Gallery, London, has prominently displayed Milne's best known sculpture, *Gnathos*, in the first room containing Patrick Heron's colourful stained glass window.

The numbing depression with which Milne was afflicted during the final weeks of his life, when he withdrew and failed to keep in touch with even his closest friends, was no doubt exacerbated by sleeping pills. He attributed some of his problems to his 'parent's total lack of compatability', and, by extension, to the general indifference of their attitude to John's chosen profession. In late June 1978, a day after his birthday, he was found dead at the bottom of the main stairs in Trewyn House. He was 47. The inquest reached a verdict of accidental death. He was taking sleeping pills in order to relax on the day of his death.

Writing Milne's 'Obituary' in The Times, E.H. Ramsden observed that at the time of his 'premature' death Milne was 'at the height of his powers and in the midst of preparing a second large scale exhibition for America later this year.' '[21] Sadly an exhibition in California, when it did come, at the Gallery Rose in Los Angeles in October 1980, was a memorial one. Ramsden concluded that Milne was 'an artist of acute sensibility, too acute perhaps for his own contentment'. There is no doubt that Milne's work has given, and will continue to give, contentment to an informed audience who are capable of appreciating the sculptural integrity and constructive purpose of an acutely sensitive artist.

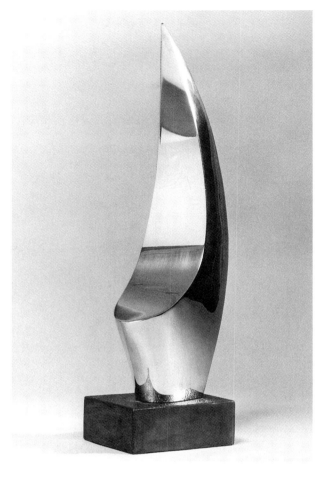

John Milne *Cybele* (1974). Polished Bronze.

FOOTNOTES:

1. From the artist's private, unpublished notes. 18/2/71. Courtesy Brian Smith, St. Ives.
2. ibid.
3. Bernard Denvir. 'London Letter', 'Studio International.' Vol.XV1/5. 20/5/72.
4. Brian Smith in conversation with the author, St. Ives. May 1999.
5. Artist's notes, Undated.
6. ibid.
7. Bryan Robertson.
8. Bryan Robertson. Plymouth retrospective exhibition catalogue. 1971.
9. J.P. Hodin 'Some Art Historical Aspects of John Milne's latest works.' Introduction to exhibition catalogue, Marjorie Parr Gallery, 4-26 Oct. 1974.
10. Artist's notes. Feb. 1978.
11. Hodin. Marjorie Parr Gallery, Oct. 1974.
12. 'Herald Tribune' (New York) 19/10/74.
13. Michael Goedhuis. 'Studio International'. Nov. 1974.
14. Denis Brown. 'Arts Review'. Oct. 1974.
15. Artist's notes. Feb. 1978.
16. Tommy Rowe in telephone conversation with the author, 10/8/99.
17. From the artist's notes, Feb. 1978.
18. ibid.
19. ibid.
20. 'Saltram Carves A "Coup" '. 'Western Morning News'. 11/6/77.
21. E.H. Ramsden. Obituary of John Milne. 'The Times'. 3/7/78.

6

Roger Leigh:
The Architect Sculptor

Roger Leigh (1925-97), the son of a landed Gloucestershire farmer, made an important, and as yet not fully recognised, contribution to sculpture in the west country. He also practised as an architect and from 1966 taught sculpture at Exeter College of Art, now part of the University of Plymouth. His keen knowledge of, and interest in, modern studio ceramics led in his late work to a novel and often humorous fusion of the sculptural and ceramic traditions. Indeed his interest in the links between architecture, design, sculpture and pottery made him an ideal teacher in art school environments where basic design, inter-disciplinary approaches and other post-Bauhaus methods were the order of the day.

During the war, while serving in the RAF, Leigh attended life drawing classes at the Ruskin School in Oxford. Once out of uniform he succumbed to family pressure and entered the architecture department of Liverpool University, where he studied Architecture and Planning between 1947 and 1953. He attended life drawings classes run on Saturday mornings by the painter Arthur Ballard at the municipal college of art. Leigh also used the college to learn about pottery, and threw his first pots under the guidance of Stan English. Together with study of architecture and landscape design these skills would be as fitting a preparation for his later vocation as would a conventional academic training in sculpture.

Contacts between architecture and art students were indeed encouraged. Leigh recalled the importance of one art student, Jane Priestman, who as well as becoming an early girlfriend later distinguished herself by becoming a design director for British Rail and British Airways. Leigh's earliest sculpture-making ventures were, however, limited to vacations, when he carved small wood figures using trees from his family's large grounds at Broadwell in Gloucestershire. Using elm, cherry and mulberry and bearing such titles as *Seated Figure* (1951) and *Family Group* (1952) these early stylised figures were unmistakeably inspired by Henry Moore, whose work he saw in the open air at the 1948 Battersea Park sculpture exhibition.

Seeing contemporary sculpture at Battersea Park was important since literature on modern art was scarce. Liverpool College of Art barely had a sculpture facility at the time though the city possessed many fine Victorian statues, particularly in St. Johns Gardens near to the Walker Art Gallery, which itself owned a collection of white marble neo-classical figures. The broader look at modern British sculpture afforded by the Battersea Park displays encouraged Leigh, who at the time was on his way to Venice on a University trip. The sensitive placement of sculpture by Moore, Hepworth and many others among the trees, plants and open spaces of the park undoubtedly struck a chord in the mind of a student already well versed in the practical and aesthetic principles of landscape design, town planning and the relationship of architecture to the broader environment in general.

Of an even greater significance than Battersea Park was the Festival of Britain in 1951. The Festival established a vision for the future and stressed the relevance of good modern design across all aspects of life. A similar spirit existed among the artists and craftsmen of St. Ives, who collaborated frequently. As his student period drew to a close Leigh looked beyond Liverpool and his meeting Barbara Hepworth at the Tate Gallery opening for the Unknown Political Prisoner exhibition in 1952 proved to be crucial for determining his future. Leigh's architectural background was a perceived advantage, Hepworth relying on loyal and practically adept assistants who would not confuse their own artistic ambitions with the particular demands and rigours of a busy workshop. Leigh was offered employment and he moved to St. Ives not long after graduating from Liverpool.

Barbara Hepworth with a group of her sculptures in the grounds of Trewyn Studios.

Leigh's integration into the close-knit but competitive art colony was rapid. As well as guaranteeing a vital income, association with Hepworth helped open doors. It encouraged his own modest sculpture output, which he was able to exhibit at the Penwith Society. Though unwilling to share professional contacts - Leigh later recalling that Hepworth's 'greenhouse was opaque with white-wash... her 'unmentioned' or 'unmentionable' assistants were thus invisible to a V.I.P '[1] - Hepworth did pull strings to further the careers of her assistants. She helped Leigh into the Penwith Society, oversaw his rise to full membership and later to the chairmanship itself. Hepworth clearly trusted and respected him. In a reference written for him in 1954 she spoke of 'a most creative person and a fine sculptor and

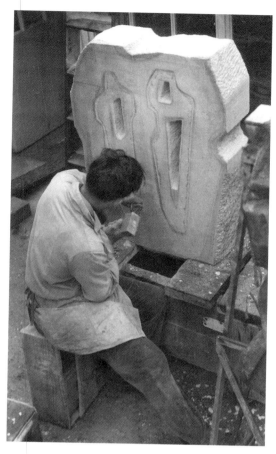

Roger Leigh
carving Barbara
Hepworth's
Hieroglyph (1953).

craftsman... a highly developed social sensibility.' [2] Her high opinion had not changed five years later when she wrote to John Milne that as Penwith chairman 'Roger is excellent...'. [3]

The precision jobs consigned to the assistants included mundane, as well as creatively challenging, tasks. The skillful, painstaking job of roughing out large carvings like the limestone *Hieroglyph* (1953) required 'the greatest sense of responsibility and enthusiasm' [4] qualities Hepworth specifically attributed to him. Less sleight of hand was required for chores that Leigh remembered included 'looking for her lost black cat for half a day... wrapping palm trees in her garden with newspaper to protect from winter frosts... clipping her laurel hedge.' [5] He was even sent to London with Denis Mitchell, where they spent several weeks preparing for Hepworth's important retrospective exhibition at the Whitechapel Art Gallery in the spring of 1954.

Influenced by high professional standards at Trewyn, Leigh continued his explorations of wood carving, which remained modest in scale and tied to figure or animal subjects. They impressed Hepworth, who visited Leigh's small cottage in Hicks Court, an enclave off the Digey, a pedestrian link between the harbour front and Porthmeor. The Cottage, rented from Denis Mitchell's brother, Endell, became Leigh's first studio. Working at home as a sideline to a paid occupation would remain the pattern for the rest of his career. Unable to devote undivided attention to sculpture alone he at least worked in areas immediately adjacent or relevant to it. This was true in London, where he worked for a couple of years as an architect with the London County Council, designing old people's homes and warehouses.

The years 1955 and 1956 yielded a group of sculptures that transcended the early influence of Moore and reflected his year spent in Trewyn Studio. The inevitable influence of Hepworth was registered in more streamlined abstract shapes like the carrara *Pierced Dolman* (1955), the walnut *White Cleft* or the mulberry *Maritime Form II* (1956). Carved in his Chelsea flat, these abstract sculptures were meticulously finished, the latter following the example of Hepworth's well known 'Pelagos' (1946) in painting an interior depression with white. *Counterthrust* (1957) prised from a single volume of laurel, embodied considerable variations of surface direction, the top of the sculpture appearing to twist across the curve of the lower part. With its many facets *Counterthrust* possessed a sculptural compactness that also needed viewing from many directions. The year *Counterthrust* was carved Leigh returned to Cornwall. Employment in London earned him enough money to buy a small cottage 'Boscampys', at Nancledra, between St. Ives and Penzance.

Hepworth was particularly pleased by his return; he once again worked for her on a part time basis. He used the Nancledra base to expand his activities. 'I made my first garden from scratch round my cottage - a furtherance of interest in landscape design from Liverpool.' '6 This outdoor space encouraged him to tackle larger scale, a factor that surfaced in his work in wood, stone and metal during the 1960s. The influence of the Penwith landscape beyond his garden also had an impact, his limestone stack *Fivestones* (1962) echoing the primitive construction of the quoits and standing stones strewn across the moors above his house. A romantic streak was evident in the large stone or wood sculptures; created specifically for a permanent outdoor setting they were subject to weathering and other processes of natural decay. The artist seemed to encourage the hand of nature and time, factors that highlighted the perhaps intended transitoriness of his non-domestic 'oeuvre'.

The remote position of the Penwith peninsular did not isolate Leigh from either the St. Ives or London art worlds. He was visited at Nancledra by Philip James, Director of visual arts at the Arts Council. In 1958 his work was exhibited in '4 and 2' at the Drian Gallery in central London. Waddington Gallery held his work and in 1964 he enjoyed a solo show at Denis Bowen's New Vision Centre Gallery. Enjoying the mobility that ownership of a car provided, Leigh taught

Roger Leigh
Counterthrust
(1957) Laurel.

Roger Leigh
Untitled (1961)
Bronze. Exhibited
New Vision Centre
1964.

architecture and town planning in Camborne. He also taught on foundation studies at Falmouth College of Art. Shortly before leaving Cornwall in 1966 he even practised again as an architect in Truro, assisting on a part time basis in the firm of John Crowther and Associates.

The early 1960s was a busy and important time. As well as acting as chairman of the Penwith Society (1959-61) Leigh received several sculpture commissions. *Iridos*, a bronzed wood composition of soaring elements, was placed at Bishops School, Chester, in 1964. The following year, as if to acknowledge an early Liverpool background, Mutley Properties in Bootle commissioned *Sagitta II* (1965), another large, thrusting, angular composition that the artist recalled 'was a fine piece of re-inforced concrete casting in dark red/brown cement.' [7] The sculpture's extruding 'limbs', articulating but not enclosing space, echoed the building's structural 'stilts' in perhaps too explicit a way. The powerful structural slant of such commissioned pieces characterised his work of the period, which assembled elements in rhythmically dynamic sequences. *Birdflight* (1960) reached across space as it dangled from a tree.

The romantic overtones of Leigh's sculpture entered into his handling of metal. *Bridle Couple* (1961) and *Two Figures on a Beach* (1964) witnessed a whimsical use of steel fragments to construct primitive upright figures. *Steel Germination* (1965) went further, a surreal-like tableau of mysterious elements evoking both hard geometry and soft biomorphic forms. Leigh conjured 'organic' imagery from the material of steel and brass, *Stamen* (1964) composed of looming petal-like forms. The leit-motif of flowering and natural growth yielded *Flowerhead* (1965) shortly after, a stained timber assemblage of densely bunched elements. Even in bronzes such as the thin stem-like cast *Axil* (1964) the theme of organic growth is evoked through bud-like forms.

Roger Leigh
Flowerhead (1965)
Stained wood.

'At the time of *Axil*', Leigh explained, 'I was very much into organic plant-inspired sculpture... the 'chevrons' were a motif implying movement or 'buds' in this case. (The chevron motif has been with me for most of my working life)... as in arrowheads they represent movement - a theme that has always been in my work up to the 80s.' [8] This depiction of movement later took on a literal guise, kinetic or mobile structures placed outdoors and bending this way or that according to wind direction.

57

The outdoor orientation of much of Leigh's work found perfect outlet during the summer of 1970 when he displayed three large wood structures in the exhibition 'Ten Sculptors, Two Cathedrals' at Winchester and Salisbury cathedrals. He also exhibited in 'Shapes in Spaces' at the Woburn Park Garden Centre in Bedfordshire and in 'Sculpture and Ceramics for Out of Doors' at the Marjorie Parr Gallery. Among the three pieces contributed to the Winchester and Salisbury displays, *Diamond Discharge* and *Portico* (1969) achieved an equilibrium between contained and bursting energy. The former's defining lozenge framed four thick wood sections tilting in assorted directions. The illusion of pictorial enclosure was belied by the actual spatial extension of these squat railway sleeper elements. In *Portico* a 'wigwam' stack of long wood beams only partially enclosed space. The scale and powerful directional slant of *Portico*

Roger Leigh *Diamond Discharge* (1965) Stained timber.

drew attention to the stone structure of the cathedral through a thrusting 'signpost' element. Michael Pennie wrote that the sculpture exhibited outside Winchester Cathedral 'must be of a size and scale to survive the distractions of the surrounding architecture.' [9] The reviewer of the concurrent Woburn exhibition, Conway Lloyd Morgan, wrote that Leigh's 'otherwise delightful' [10] *Rhomb* was not given a sufficiently clear space to do itself justice, a factor proving the powerful architectonic - and indeed environmental - dimension of Leigh's sculpture.

Leigh exhibited *Flatsider* (1969) at the Marjorie Parr exhibition. A notable example of his powerful, robust compositions in stained timber, *Flatsider* was the product of skillful carpentry and sensitive placement of

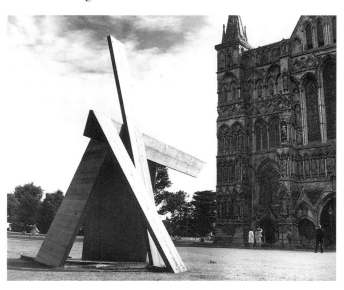

abstract wood sections along lateral and vertical axes. The abstraction of *Flatsider* pleased Brian Hornal who wrote that 'the overwhelming lesson of the outdoors is that form (as scale modulation) must dominate any obvious content.' [11] The critical criterion of sculptural

Roger Leigh *Portico* (1969) Wood. Pictured outside Winchester Cathedral 1970.

58

scale - particularly in relation to buildings or the landscape - drove Leigh to make ambitious structures that dwarfed human scale.

The environmental scale of *Portico* was emulated by *Pierced Pallisade*, a large fence-like structure commissioned for the grounds of an architect, Peter Wakefield, at Warminster. A site-specific sculpture placed against a looming tree at the top of a long pathway, *Pallisade* cut a fan-like profile of vertical wood elements bolted to low-lying structural chevrons snaking around the base of the vertical members. Similar site-specific criteria were used for the extended steel sculpture *Partition* (1969-71), which, like *Pallisade* acted as a shaping element in dividing and defining a given landscape setting. In this instance a rectilinear composition of mild steel plate was designed along the curvature of a piece of landscape design between Devonshire House and the Queens Building on the campus of the University of Exeter.

Above: Roger Leigh *Flatsider* (1969) Stained timber.

Roger Leigh *Partition* (1969) Steel. University of Exeter.

The artist's use of open space as an equal compositional element with solid volume yielded a sculpture in which a pathway traversed the work. Large scale modern sculpture had often flirted with the idea of human entry and here Leigh uses the functional, as well as aesthetic, disciplines of landscape design, town planning and sculpture-making to invest the notion with literal proportion. *Partition* was bought on commission by the University of Exeter in 1971 with aid of an Arts

Council grant. The product of carefully prepared designs and a balsawood model, *Partition* is composed from eight units of steel plate painted and zinc primed. The orange and green colour of the surfaces reflect specific landscape features such as the grass lawn while the irregular planes of bent and folded rectangular plate creates what the artist described as 'varying interplay of light.' [12] The 'romantic' concern with light reflected the work's intended merging with both man-made and natural features of the surroundings.

The outdoor orientation of Leigh's experimental works took the form, from 1968 onwards, of temporary structures in nylon fabric. Inspired by flags and yacht sails experienced on sailing expeditions during the 1950s, these fabric sheets were suspended in space on strings or steel cables. The translucent colours of the fabrics fulfilled Leigh's interest in colouristic side-effects, enabling the works to become, in the artist's words, 'variable paintings in space, motionless or in violent movement - the form, colour, tones changing according to weather conditions.' [13] The product of elevated and exposed six-acre grounds around his home 'Sorbus' in Aldbourne, Wiltshire - to where he had moved from Cornwall in 1966 these makeshift, light structures gave expression to the often violent winds that swept across the Marlborough Downs. Leigh designed a large but temporary mural in nylon sheet for the facade of Exeter College of Art. Extending from the wall of the college building - rather than wrapping or enclosing it in the manner of Christo - this relief-like structure was essentially a decorative embellishment. A more conventional sculpture reading was provided by *Wind Pivot* (1971) a free-standing, if kinetic, object composed with nylon wrapped around steel or bamboo. True to its title *Wind Pivot* turned on a pair of steel 'spindles' its pair of vertical and horizontal 'sails' utilising wind direction, to which it bent back and forth.

Roger Leigh *Wind Pivot* (1971) Nylon steel and bamboo.

Leigh's move to 'Sorbus', an architect-designed modern movement house, reflected his involvement with architecture. Designed in 1931 by the architect T.S. Tait, 'Sorbus's white rectangle was one of the earliest examples of its kind in Britain. Its proportioned classicism reflected the Bauhaus principles that Leigh, in spite of his rather eccentric involvement with kinetic structures open to the natural elements, taught at Exeter College of Art as well as during occasional visits to Reading University and Winchester School of Art. Many of the structural and formal principles used in his sculptures derived from

Sorbus Leigh's house on Marlborough Downs.

Roger Leigh posturing with a ceramic sculpture, mid 1990s.

Kandinsky and Mondrian, the former's theoretical text 'Point and Line to a Plane' proving particularly relevant to the directional lines, chevrons and distribution of heavy and grounded or light and air-bound elements in his three dimensional work.

Leigh and his wife Pat remained in Wiltshire. He taught at Exeter on a part-time basis until retirement in the mid 1980s. He moved from 'Sorbus' to 'Overhollow' a large nineteenth-century house at Erlestoke, near Westbury. His final domicile, 'Tackles Barn' at Marden, near Devizes, saw Leigh produce many ceramic sculptures based on the shapes of alphabetical letters and fired at the kiln of Exeter College of Art. Living at Marden from the early 1990s until his death in 1997, Leigh became reclusive, only managing to see an old Cornish colleague, Michael Canney, on one occasion. Canney had moved back from Italy in 1993 and lived in nearby Devizes. Canney's wallbound coloured reliefs, seamless constructions of wedgelike wood components, bear a striking resemblence to the free-standing forms Leigh made in the 1960s.

The late fired ceramic forms witness an artist in lighthearted, humorous mood. They provide an opportunity to posit literary references within a tough, uncompromising, formal and architectonic language. Leigh's *Homage to Gaudi* once again reflected his knowledge of, and admiration for, the finest architectural achievements of given times and places. His admiration for another Spaniard, the sculptor Eduardo Chillida, was registered in more plastic terms than the ceramic *Homage to Gaudi*. The particular gravitas and shaping of space through lumpen form that is a feature of Chillida's work informs Leigh's late ceramic pieces. Although these are neat, coherent typographic structures they employ the same pertinent dialogue between open spaces and enclosed shapes characteristic of Chillida and of his own earlier sculpture. The ceramic sculptures hark back to Leigh's lifelong interest in pottery, stemming from early studies of the subject while a student in Liverpool. The use of colour to finish the fired works provide a pictorial embellishment and a reminder that, in spite of his manual craftsmanship, he was a fine artist working in dialogue with painters like Canney, as well as with sculptors.

FOOTNOTES:

1. Roger Leigh. Letter to the author. 27/1/91.
2. Barbara Hepworth. Reference letter 13/7/54. Courtesy Nicholas Leigh.
3. Barbara Hepworth. Letter to John Milne. 15/2/59. Courtesy Brian Smith, St. Ives.
4. Hepworth. 13/7/54.
5. Leigh to the author. 7/6/93.
6. ibid.
7. Leigh to the author. 27/1/91.
8. Leigh to the author. 7/6/93.
9. Michael Pennie. 'Outdoor Sculpture'. 'Arts Review' .p.461. July 1970.
10. Conway Lloyd Morgan. 'Outdoor Sculpture'. 'Arts Review' p.461. 1970.
11. Brian Hornal. 'Outdoor Sculpture' 'Arts Review' 1970.
12. Roger Leigh interviewed by Christopher Lane. BBC TV. 1971.
13. Roger Leigh. 'Ariel Wind Sculpture in Nylon Fabric 1968'. 'One' magazine. April 1974.

7

Brian Wall:
Three Dimensional Mondrians

Modern sculpture's appropriation of new technological and industrial materials and use of constructional processes, once the preserve of engineering, sidestepped the traditional distinction between modelled and carved categories. Mid twentieth century critics like Adrian Stokes and Herbert Read - the example of Picasso, Gonzalez and Smith notwithstanding - saw sculpture as belonging to one or other category. Constructivism's use of new materials enabled direct collaging. Open space played a more vital role in the work, replacing the solid volume of monolithic sculpture. The process of welding or forging - as to opposed to casting - proved liberating, giving artists license to add or subtract elements as part of an open-ended or ongoing process. Herbert Read wrote that the 'malleable process' of metal construction had 'decisive virtues for sculpture.'

Centering on technical considerations these distinctions do not deal directly with matters of style, content or meaning. The division between figurative and abstract also breaks down; all sculpture is in a sense abstract while even the most extreme geometric forms of sculpture enter an unavoidable dialogue with either the scale or specific form of the human figure, landscape or architecture. The critic R.H. Wilenski used the term 'architectural' to denote 'formal': for him this category is not only about buildings but about qualities of structure, materials and use of space that distinguishes both architecture and free-standing sculpture at its best.

The British-born sculptor Brian Wall embarked on an artistic career in the mid 1950s. His sculpture has always been 'architectural', sometimes even in the literal sense. Early constructions, open, upright and box-like, were akin to architectural models. Painted in enamel paints these wood structures were the product of a young artist who had started as a painter. *Metamorphosis* (1955), extended rectangles of primary colour into the third dimension. He described these early works as like 'three dimensional Mondrians', coloured rectangles of wood or steel standing in plan or elevation on rectilinear scaffolds. But Ben Nicholson also was an influence, particularly Nicholson's introduction of a shallow, carved space in his white reliefs.

Wall made acquaintance with Nicholson in St. Ives, Cornwall, where the young Wall had moved in 1954. The eager London-born artist's entry into the competitive art colony went well and he began working as assistant to Barbara Hepworth, with Henry Moore the pre-eminent sculptor in Britain. Perhaps Wall's smooth entry had something to do with maturity, having learnt a trade and having travelled widely during two years National Service in the RAF. On the advice of a poet friend, Bob Cobbing, he decided to become an artist and go to St. Ives. He was determined and full of confidence. The painter Robert Brennan, whom Wall later described as a 'keystone', introduced him to the artists in the town. One of the best of them, the Constructivist-influenced landscape painter Peter Lanyon - who had also served in the RAF and made make-shift sculptures and three dimensional objects as a preparation for paintings - encouraged Wall. He helped the recruit find a small studio in the middle of town near to the harbour front.

But the chief catalyst in Brian Wall's early development was the period working for Barbara Hepworth in St. Ives. From a superficial stylistic viewpoint Wall's sculpture has seldom appeared to owe much to Hepworth. Yet the invaluable experience of the Trewyn years makes it appropriate to speak of a Hepworth influence. In her studio Wall learnt a professional code, one where single-minded dedication and sensitivity to materials went hand in hand with a powerful aesthetic rationale. Working for her not only integrated him with the St. Ives artist's community, in particular giving him a working accord with other young sculptors and craftsmen similarly employed - Denis Mitchell, Roger Leigh, Keith Leonard and the furniture maker Dicon Nance among them - but provided a glimpse into the machinations of the British art establishment. Association with

Brian Wall on Porthmeor Beach c.1957.

Hepworth may not have necessarily guaranteed the success of his own work, but it certainly lent a professional status.

Wall harnassed the influence to positive, rather than vicarious, ends. He belonged to a younger generation who shared a different set of technical and aesthetic priorities. The critic Lawrence Alloway put the point clearly when he wrote that 'none of the pre-war British artists are important for non-figurative art: they have either become romantics or, like Nicholson and Hepworth at least tired of their thirtyish purity.' [1] One of the technical interests pursued by Wall's generation was the use of steel, as opposed to more traditional materials, with which to construct sculpture. Though personal and empirical, Wall's preference for steel gave his work a contemporary feel that enabled him to react against the modelling and carving modes favoured by Hepworth, Moore and other pre-war sculptors.

In spite of never feeling as comfortable with metals Hepworth was, however, using them extensively in her work by the mid 1950s. She was making curvilinear pieces from thin sheets of brass or copper, 'Stringed figure (Curlew)' and 'Forms in movement (Gilliard)' being 1956 examples, or else casting earlier plasters in bronze. Sculptures like 'Cantate Domino', 'Sea Form (Porthmeor)' or 'Miridian' - all made in 1958 - witnessed a use of bronze casting on a larger, more public scale. Wall worked on the plaster and post-cast stages of 'Meridian', a notable Hepworth sculpture originally sited at State House in central London. Wall's expertise, gained as a glass blower in Hertfordshire, as an aircraft engineer in the RAF, and as a steel welder, made him an ideal, not to say timely, recruit at Trewyn. His acquired skills were a timely asset for the development of his own work, too. With them he experimented with a potent mixture of discipline and abandon.

The industrial connotations of Wall's chosen sculptural method seemed at odds with the 'organic', hand craft tradition of St. Ives. While anticipating future artistic development in an urban context, Wall's elegant, spare use of steel plate in fact contributed to St. Ives art as a whole. Within the inclusive colony craftsmen had traditionally shared an elevated creative platform with fine artists. The successful establishment of the Leach pottery two decades before modern art started in earnest in Cornwall witnessed the equal partnership of craft and fine art. No single process was considered inferior to another, and while technical accomplishment was considered important, one did not have to be experienced or academically trained to be seen as artistically relevant. The development of an authentic personal voice within a pluralistic artistic milieu, therefore grew as much from an honest, - and in Wall's case unique - engagement with materials as from sharing in current, often ideological, approaches to abstraction.

Denis Mitchell's humble beginnings as a local craftsman who gradually matured into an independent sculptor was a case in point. As Hepworth's chief studio assistant throughout the 1950s, he recommended Wall join her working team. Mitchell also pointed him to evening classes in welding at Camborne School of Art. Equipped thereafter with sound knowledge of steel welding, Wall began making his first free-standing constructions that turn a restricted vocabulary of steel plate to a distinct artistic advantage. Wall's early sculptures, while setting his work apart, reflected his acquisition of manifold skills beyond welding. Polishing or patinating bronzes, cutting copper, drilling holes in metal or else carving them in stone were all relevant tasks performed for Hepworth.

One of the notable features of Wall's 'oeuvre' - single-minded adherence to one material, steel, and one process, welding - highlights its consistency and integrity. Early St. Ives sculptures, modest in scale and deftly economic in form, conformed to a tenet central to the St. Ives 'school' and, beyond it, to an indigenous Cornish genius for making things in makeshift circumstances. Ben Nicholson had championed the unschooled paintings of the St. Ives primitive Alfred Wallis who, in old age, turned to the materials closest at hand - bits of discarded board and old tins of yacht paint - to make some of the most haunting images of the sea. Wallis's 'cult' status among modern artists exerted a moral, as well as aesthetic, influence. Cornwall's harsh and poverty-stricken past, as a barren and austere landscape on the edge of the British Isles, fostered a salutary, ingenious feeling for the ramshackle and provisional.

In like manner Wall found it necessary to make do with whatever sources for metal he could find. The sources were two scrapyards in Hayle and in Penzance which belonged to a local engineering firm, Holmans. Wall scoured these yards like an avid beachcomber. The available offcuts were varied to just five thicknesses. From this limited repertoire Wall learnt quickly to fall back on his intuition, testing the potential for diversity of expression. How far could one continue to make meaningful art from so limited a range of shapes? The answer lay in an unencumbered technique, in a realisation that space and even time could play a crucial role in the composition and in a tempering of constructive order with the delightful unpredictability of chance.

Also important in the conditioning of Wall's identity was a hunger to learn about vital and progressive sculpture in other countries. In the late 1950s 'other countries' still meant France. Armed with the potent, if limited, connections that his successful absorption into the St. Ives milieu afforded, Wall visited Paris and met two leading French sculptors, Cézar and Germaine Richier. He also visited what he described as the 'musty' and 'packed' studio of Constantin Brancusi, the great Romanian sculptor and a principal inspiration for Hepworth. The diversity of materials used by Brancusi both in individual pieces and across the entire 'oeuvre' was an object lesson in the fusion of 'low' peasant craft and sophisticated fine art production. The functional and contemplative co-existed. The Brancusi experience was more a foil than a cue, encouraging rather than diminishing Wall's belief in the advantages of a single material. But meeting Brancusi promoted the idea that even in the modern age sculpture could be a life, something Wall had, of course, already witnessed in 'atelier Hepworth'.

Wall met such eminent and famous artists with a letter of introduction from the French critic Michel Seuphor who, due to his association with Hepworth, illustrated Wall in a recent book, published by Zwemmers, 'The Sculpture of this Century' (1960). Hepworth had known the old Romanian sculptor in earlier days and David Lewis, a curator at the Penwith Gallery in St. Ives, had written a book, 'Constantin Brancusi', which was published in London in 1957. The lofty reputation of the artists he met in Paris glamorised, in the impressionable mind of a young artist, the difficult task of making modern sculpture, Wall's work did, however, differ markedly from theirs. Cézar's, for example, used mythic or literary imagery in a way that Wall's would never; Richier belonged to a tradition of figurative French sculpture stretching back to Bourdelle, Dalou and Rodin while Brancusi's effect was at once inimitable and unavoidable. The chief benefit of the visit was to provide an encouraging cosmopolitan perspective. However diverse sculpture in Britain had become much of it was derivative or inferior. The work of Michael Ayrton, for example, seemed a pale reflection of Cézar's, while Armitage, Frink and Chadwick, among the younger generation in Britain, followed the distorted styles of Richier and Giacometti. Given Wall's later move to the United States, where his work developed in a transatlantic context, such early experiences in the Parisian melting pot cannot be irrelevant.

While the term 'constructivist' can be broadly applied to Wall's work, his interpretation of the word led to very different outcomes from that of Hepworth. Hepworth's sculpture continued to contain references to the figure, or to figure-in-the-landscape. This was true even in the open and pierced forms, like 'Pelagos' (1946), which were derived from the pure cones or spheres of the 1930s. Residual landscape content contrasted with Wall's slim, open linear structures that, while eschewing any symbolic possibilities, literary references or theatrical associations, contained an implied pictoriality. This pictoriality was not representational in kind but adhered to abstract principles such as the movement of lines between points in space. By speaking of 'three dimensional Mondrians', Wall declared a plastic synthesis of form and colour, not on the flat, four-sided surface of de Stijl painting, but within the sculptor's domain of real three dimensional space. The early freestanding wood construction *Right Angle Deck Construction with Vertical Movement* had the further feature of resembling a furniture object or item of utility, fulfilling the de Stijl movement's desire to include functional, everyday objects in its neo-plastic design revolution.

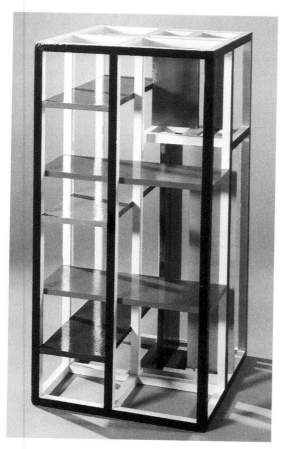

Brian Wall *Right Angle Deck Construction*. Painted wood (1956).

In *Deck Construction* Wall indeed manages to link painting and sculpture. But whereas pictorial space is illusionistic in *Deck Construction* it becomes a real, concrete agent. Planes painted red, orange and green are 'floors' of a rectilinear 'tower'. White and black scaffolding defines the outer 'wall' of a vertical 'box'. The conventional distinction between architecture, furniture, painting and sculpture breaks down. But Wall's intention is wholly sculptural, an intention made clear after 1956 when he replaced wood with the altogether more durable material of steel. Subsequent sculptures, painted with a matt black paint, emphasising the uniform material with which they were made, reduced the optical and psychological side-effects of colour. The Russian Suprematist painter Kasimir Malevich used black for similar formal ends, enhancing the basic constituent forms - squares, circles and crosses - from which his uncompromising compositions were constructed. By dismantling the recurring box format, replacing its rectilinarity with the unpredictable rhythms of slanting elements moving in random directions, Wall introduced space as an active, vital component. Nonetheless, a kind of residual adherence to the open box - and indeed to the figure of the human participator - was maintained by ascentric lines that extended no further than arm's length. In this way the composition, though extended in a multiplicity of spatial directions, retained the graspable dimension of a solid object.

Wall's awareness of relevant contemporaries working on the continent and, before them, of pre-war modernist pioneers like Malevich and Mondrian, was tempered by the more direct inspiration of local artists in St. Ives. With them he shared practical, as well as ideological, concerns. One of the most influential at the time was John Forrester, described by Wall as important for him in what was a vital transitional period 'because he allowed me to intellectually bridge the gap' between painting and sculpture. Painting was in fact decreed by Wall to be 'not quite adequate physically'. The fact that sculpture and painting often shared a common aesthetic purpose did not diminish their intrinsic differences. The seemingly hard, intractable nature of steel was belied by its constructional versatility, lending the medium a clay or plaster-like malleability. The slow rigour of carpentry was replaced by the more spontaneous and improvisatory procedure that welding allowed.

The sculptures that Wall produced in a studio he shared with the painter Trevor Bell at Wheal Dream (a quiet street near the 'Island' at the back of the town) were linear, rather than directly planar, in quality. This reflected the kind of steel then obtainable in Cornwall. Only towards the end of the 1950s, when his early St. Ives career was drawing to a close, did Wall introduce into his sculpture a more varied range of steel plate and offcut. Compositionally, the sculptures varied from the relative minimalism of *Maquette For Standing Form X* (1958), which possesses the graphic simplicity of calligraphy, to the denser web of *Landscape Sculpture* or *Untitled* of the same year.

The theme of diversity-within-unity reflects Wall's interest in the work of another Russian painter, Wassily Kandinsky, a pioneer of abstract painting and a distinguished teacher at the Bauhaus. The contradictory spaces and shifting perspectival foci Kandinsky used in the 'Composition' and 'Improvisation' series of the early Munich period appealed to Wall who, in his St. Ives constructions, created the same brittle tension between containment and fragmentation, between the disequilibrium of parts and the cohesion of the whole. Kandinsky's Bauhaus book 'Point and Line to a Plane' (1926) provided a theoretical framework for artists who, like Wall and Leigh, were committed to keeping their language plain, simple and geometric. The importance of using reason and intuition, order and chance in the working process accorded with Kandinsky's dictum that a finished artwork be a perfect synthesis between 'inner necessity' and outer expressiveness. Simple principles about the relative psychological, visual and formal effects of compositional disposition lent the work of abstract artists a universal power exceeding that generated within the confines of conventional figurative art.

In Kandinsky's thinking the static points and moving lines created tensions in relation to the four sides of a given plane. In the third dimension of sculpture, however, such lines could advance or recede in actual, as opposed to graphic, space, and in so doing introduce not only real space but an element of time. The viewer needed time in order to walk around the object and experience it from all directions.

It is of course doubtful whether Wall ever observed, or would have wanted to observe, a doctrinaire aesthetic programme. Contemporary artists like Kenneth and Mary Martin, John Ernest or Victor Anton, were more prone to pursuing systematic or mathematic possibilities. If the English sculptor's work is notable for its complete abstraction, where any literary or symbolic intentions are emphatically denied, then Kandinsky's interest in the analogy between music and abstract art was relevant to a form of sculpture flowing with formal and spatial movement. Formal engineering is also manifestly at play in Wall's sculpture. Resting on a small steel 'plinth' or horizontal plane which functions both structurally and aesthetically, Wall's St. Ives constructions seem at once stable and precarious. The central upright steel 'armature' seldom rises as a perfect vertical. Instead it leans sideways ready to fall. But elements that extend like branches from the originating 'trunk' hold one another in a way described by the American curator George Neubert as 'a dynamic disequilirium' of constructive energy.[2] Thanks to the versatile process of welding Wall's sculpture became one where, in Neubert's words, 'Drama takes the place of equilibrium'.

Mondrian's denial of the third dimension is perhaps surprising for an artist who wrote in 'Plastic and Pure Plastic Art' that art needs 'to achieve a balance between the subjective and the objective', and who predicted that painting would one day become obsolete and overtaken by 'real' life. Given the manner that the de Stijl movement, to which Mondrian was a leading member, extended its design revolution to encompass furniture, interior design, typography and architecture, one might expect Mondrian to have produced free-standing structures. But as David Cohen has argued in a recent article on the subject[3] Mondrian's influence on the three-dimensional language of sculpture has been profound. 'He numbered such sculptors as Vantongerloo, Arp, Pevsner and Hepworth among his close acquaintances, and he was a source of great encouragement to young sculptors'. But Cohen fails to mention either Marlow Moss, Robert Adams or Brian Wall as artists who made sculpture more or less influenced by the aesthetics of the de Stijl and Constructivist movements. The former artist was in fact a respected member of Mondrian's de Stijl circle. Like Max Bill she made sculpture, extending her feeling for rhythm into the third dimension.

As curator of the Newlyn Gallery, Michael Canney commissioned Wall to construct wood plinths for an exhibition of tribal sculpture. Canney was aware of peripheral modernist pockets beyond St. Ives and wrote of Moss's 'secluded life' at Lamorna, near Cornwall's Lands End peninsular. Her professional ties to continental abstraction in general proved an attraction to those younger artists who, like Brian Wall and Michael Canney, were aware that the hedgmony enjoyed by Barbara Hepworth and Ben Nicholson at the Penwith Society of Arts in St. Ives was not a true reflection of the avant garde world at large. Accordingly, Wall visited Lamorna with the painter Michael Snow, only to find the reclusive artist was away. They looked through small studio windows and discovered canvases hanging across interior walls, a vivid, if indirect, experience that encouraged their own experiments into non-objective form as well as providing vitally important proof of an alternative to anglicised St. Ives modernism.

This episode serves to illustrate that, though greatly benefiting from his years with Hepworth, Brian Wall maintained the healthiest independence of spirit. He questioned her dominance, later speaking of an autocratic figure who would 'brook no dissent'. She respected his independence, though differences led to his leaving Trewyn Studio and relinquishing the secretaryship of the Penwith Society. He also began exhibiting his distinctive steel structures outside Cornwall, at the Drian Gallery in central London.

Wall's debut at Halima Nalecz's West End gallery was in a group show of six artists from Cornwall. There were four sculptors -Denis Mitchell, Roger Leigh and Bruce Taylor, each of whom had worked in Hepworth's atelier - and two painters, Gwen Leitch and Misome Piele. Alan Bowness wrote in the catalogue about the 'hard white clarity' of the light in Cornwall, suggesting a unity between the group. The usual romantic associations detected in St. Ives modernism - a tendency that prompted the critic Lawrence Alloway to write disparagingly that 'the landscape is so nice, nobody can quite bring themselves to leave it out of their art' - did not, though, hold true to Wall's work. Alloway's other suggestion, quoted earlier, that the younger generation had reacted against the creeping romanticism that had compromised the pre-war purism of Hepworth and Nicholson, was confirmed by Keith Sutton,who wrote that the youth of the Drian exhibitors 'might account for an interest in materials at the expense of content.'

The new constructive freedom enjoyed by Wall and his contemporaries had been pioneered by a group including Victor Pasmore, Kenneth Martin and Robert Adams, who came together after the 1951 Festival of Britain. Alloway championed them in his book 'Nine Abstract Artists' (1954). They made mobiles, reliefs and other three dimensional structures that brought them into direct collaboration with architects and interior designers. They exhibited together in Adrian Heath's Fitzroy Street studio, London and various collaborations culminated in the landmark 'This is Tomorrow' exhibition, held at the Whitechapel Art Gallery in 1956. Kenneth Martin wrote in the group's organ 'Broadsheet': 'What is generally termed 'abstract' is not to be confused with the abstraction from nature.' The American construcivist John Ernest's 'Maquette for Constructed Tower', included in 'This is Tommorrow' could not be confused with abstraction from nature. An open tower of perspex platforms within metal uprights, Ernest's architectural model was perhaps a prototype for Wall's *Deck Construction*.

Wall was younger than Heath's constructionist group, of whom only Anthony Hill was Wall's junior. The young sculptor developed in their wake, adapting a particular interest in Mondrian to the business of making upright,open, free standing sculpture. The format of an open tower is evident in his classic early welded steel structure *Sculpture 1956* which was shown in the Whitechapel Art Gallery's important 1981 exhibition 'British Sculpture of the 20th century'. In this thin, rectilinear composition horizontal and vertical axes are held in equilibrium, the open square or rectangular spaces posited by criss-crossing lines partially enclosed by three counterpoised steel sheets, painted in the primary colours favoured by the Dutch de Stijl master.

Brian Wall
Sculpture 1956
(1956). Steel.

The rectilinearity of *Sculpture 1956* took on vertical emphases in *Steel Yellow* and *40 6Y* (1958). The box format of these was soon disrupted by centrifugal sculptures like the aptly named *Bi-centric* and *Form Y 1* (1958). Whereas *Sculpture 1956* and *Steel Yellow* posited the illusion of deep space through a variety of short or long linear accents, conveying contrasting effects of diminishing perspectives, *Bi-centric* is entirely asymetric, random and ambiguous. *40 6Y's* inclusion in a 1958 Arts Council exhibition 'Contemporary British Sculpture', proved how quickly Wall's work was being recognised. A series of *Standing Form* sculptures followed in 1959, which are composed with long sheets and plane sections. In these a fitting balance is achieved between the planar and linear dimension, something that had first appeared in *Sculpture 1956*.

Marking the end of his formative St. Ives career these sculptures were exhibited at the Drian Gallery in 1959 and 1960, and later at the Grabowski Gallery in London, where he enjoyed two solo shows in 1962 and 1964. New formal developments in Wall's sculpture reflected both new imaginative strategies and the fact of having in London access to scrapyards where a greater range of offcut was available. With this Wall improvised and the introduction of sweeping curves began to counter the rectilinearity of previous work.

FOOTNOTES:

1. Lawrence Alloway. 'Nine Abstract Artists'. Tiranti, London, 1954.
2. George Neubert. 'Brian Wall. A Partial Retrospective'. Max Hutchinson Gallery, New York. April 1981.
3. David Cohen. 'Mondrian and the Third Dimension. Sculpture.' Feb. 1996. p.28-32.

8

A Natural Gravity

Wall's connections with the London art scene, forged during his St. Ives years, were consolidated through exhibitions at the Drian, Grabowski and Grosvenor galleries. The precarious task of making a living in Cornwall, compounded by the break with Hepworth, made the move to London a necessity. Looking back he later described the move as a 'time to grow up and get on with your life.' [1] London paid rich dividends, not only professionally but socially, where Wall made numerous contacts. Drinking haunts like the Queens Elm, Chelsea, or Henekeys, Portobello Road, proved instrumental. Living in west London Wall obtained vital part-time teaching at Ealing School of Art.

In the middle 1960s colleges like Ealing were introducing basic design and other Bauhaus-derived empirical teaching methods. Such liberal principles were encouraged by a colourful staff who included Roy Ascot, Denis Bowen, Peter Startup, the Cohen brothers and the well-connected Principal, William Brooker. In 1962 Wall also started teaching at the Central School of Arts and Crafts, later becoming head of the sculpture department where he guided in the new Dip A.D. course. With the help of Henry Abercrombie, Wall upgraded a rudimentary coal-fired sand foundry and introduced an invaluable lost wax casting facility. Such improvements helped maintain the Central's reputation for high craft standards. The innovative spirit of the times was tempered by adherence to traditional levels of excellence. The presence on the staff of avant garde artists like William Turnbull, Robert Adams, William Pye as well as Brian Wall ensured the college kept abreast of contemporary developments.

According to Abercrombie, Wall 'never insisted on a house style.' [2] His teaching was pragmatic rather than doctrinaire, offering contrast to Anthony Caro's regime at the Central's neighbour, St. Martins School of Art. Rather than impose his own agenda on students Wall oversaw the upgrading of essential equipment like welding gear. The practical nature of Wall's endeavour as artist and teacher saw him inspire students not ideologically but through working alongside them on the studio floor. He led by example, welding his own sculpture in the Central's workshop. On an administrative level, too, he proved effective, later serving as a chairman on the Faculty of Fine Art at the University of Berkeley, California.

The establishment of Wall's career as a prominent teacher was accompanied by an active and prestigious schedule of solo and group exhibitions. Solo shows throughout the 1960s were accompanied by important survey shows, among them the Paris Biennale in 1961 (for which he was visited in his London studio by critic Lawrence Alloway and Lilian Somerville), the Tate Gallery's 'Sculpture of the Sixties' in 1965 and the 'New British Sculpture' show held in Bristol (Wall showed two white outdoor pieces on College Green) in 1968. In 'British Sculptors 72' at the Royal Academy, London, Wall exhibited *Long Way* (1971), which occupied a large part of a room at Burlington House. *Long Way* steps beyond the discretely proportioned constructivism of his early work and embraces the environmental dimension favoured by Caro and his contemporaries. Painted yellow, *Long Way* is, like Caro's 'Prairie', a diffuse composition stretching across space. It revealed the long journey of a young St. Ives sculptor in the shadow of Barbara Hepworth, to a prominent sculptor in his own right at the epicentre of Britain's vibrant young generation as

Brian Wall *Long Way* (1971). Steel.

it had germinated during the late 1950s and matured during the 1960s. Individuality was the watchword of Wall's career; he kept an entirely separate identity from the New Generation sculptors, whose bright coloured polymorphs proved such distinctive variation on a theme laid out in the early constructed work of Anthony Caro.

Wall's exhibitions elicited favourable critical responses. According to Norbert Lynton, the introduction of new steel shapes such as diagonals, curved sections, boxes and 'hoops' or other whittled down square forms, had 'the effect of setting into motion forms and relationships that had been tensed but static' in Wall's previous sculpture. [*3] Lynton also admired the 'atmosphere of seriousness' which was achieved, at least in part, by the absence of colour or other formal distractions. Lynton was right to point out the new sense of movement entering Wall's London sculpture. These works, which mark an extension of his technical and artistic powers, stack shapes in increasingly playful and unpredictable arrangements. *Upright Figure* (Whitford Fine Art, London) *Boxed Jenny, Two Boxes* (1962) or *Sculpture 9* (1963) continue to use the box format, which has now become whittled down allowing uprights to thrust through. Within the vertical box-like confinement of *Upright Figure* rectangular elements are tilted and slanted, creating a conflicting sense of pirouette and movement.

Maquette II (1961) and *Small Construction* (1962), by contrast, are open compositions that express space through stereometric projection. This projection is upright and totemic, rectangular steel plate stacked at right angles to the one below.

New opportunities in London meant that Wall could, for the first time, stockpile steel. This created a ready-made source from which he could improvise during the working process. 'Found' elements were intermingled with pre-cut ones in the same sculpture. As a result the sculptures increased in scale, their forms becoming heavier and often extending further into space. Alert to the danger of sinking into a 'style' or formula Wall continued to work intuitively, honouring his remarkably mature 1959 dictum that making sculpture was an exploration of the unconscious which arises from working without preconceived ideas. Working from his imagination has yielded a discrete body of work, distinct from the primary structures of the American minimalists and from the grandiloquent gestures of Caro or Richard Serra. Wall has explained his career as akin to 'a spiritual path' not one to do with religion or other organised rituals, but an 'innate, marvellous way of living'. [*4]

Brian Wall *Upright Figure* (1962). Steel.

Despite the insistent verticality of early 1960s assemblages like *Boxed Jenny*, *Two Curves* or *Upright Figure* the trend by the middle of the decade had shifted towards the horizontal. Lateral compositions, painted in a single colour were placed straight on the floor, a gesture that engaged the sculpture in a dynamic relationship with the architecture of the room while also related it to the space inhabited by the spectator. Wall's early intention that sculpture 'should be an integral part of the landscape and should not overpower, or be overpowered by natural environments' was fulfilled in these sculptures. But compared to the work of Anthony Caro, who had risen to prominence after his successful Whitechapel Art Gallery retrospective in 1963, Wall's sculpture used a scale that ensured continued kinship to the figure. Caro's early masterpieces like 'Early One Morning' (1962) or 'Prairie', by contrast, were environmental in scale and used bright, eye-catching surface colour. Wall preferred quieter constructive harmonies and a more intimate, 'European' feeling that the work should function as a coherent object true to itself and not overpowering.

images and easy graphic designs in space. None of these criticisms applied to Wall who, while lagging behind the reputations of Caro and King, enjoyed almost unanimous critical endorsement. R.C. Kennedy's description of 'ornamental leanings' *[11] in Wall's deft formal juggles with geometry suggested a kinship to a central sculptural tradition, rather than a current vogue for flat, decorative 'pictorial' shapes.

Nonetheless, a trio of recent pieces - *Maquette V*, *Round Oak* and *Untitled II* (1968) - from the Grosvenor exhibition used a 'flat' language of cut, bent or shaped planes to define space in terms of inflected steel sheet rather than solid volume. According to the critic G.S. Whittet these slanting elements seemed 'to be a means of defining space as much as occupying it.' The heavy substance of metal was alleviated by a use of flat discs, parallel to the floor, which generated a counter effect of weightlessness. The centrepiece of the Grosvenor exhibition, the twenty foot long *Two Elements*, shared with 1965 sculptures like *Four Elements*, *Brown Bomber* and *Two Discs* a belief in large scale, lateral extension and simple but powerful tube, plane and circle forms.

By the end of the 1960s Wall had consolidated, both through cogent teaching and an impressive series of group and solo exhibitions, a solid reputation at the forefront of Britain's much respected modern sculpture 'school'. Wall's achievements proved an effective launching pad for the American years that would follow his permanent move across the Atlantic in 1972. That followed a transitional period when the artist taught on both sides of the Atlantic.

Brian Wall *Right On*
1970. Steel.

From 1969 onwards Wall visited the United States every year, where he taught at summer schools or on a part time basis at the University of Berkeley, California, his eventual employer. The title of a 1970 piece, *Right On* used the language of Haight Ashbury 'cool', reflecting the fact that Wall produced the sculpture in California. In 1971 he spent as much as half his year on the West Coast, returning to the Central School to help out after the retirement of the painter Morris Kestleman. Wall encouraged American students to enter the Holborn-based college. His teaching commitments were such that during 1971 he exhibited only twice - both in Californian rather than British galleries - a situation that, coupled with his subsequent marriage to a London based American student, Sylvia Brown, confirmed his future as an American artist. His valedictory appearance in the 'British Sculptors 72' exhibition at the Royal Academy was in fact his last contribution to a major survey of contemporary British sculpture. His contribution to the Royal Academy; *Long Way*, was, however, displayed at the Silver Jubilee exhibition in Battersea Park in 1977.

Wall's undiminished position in British sculpture of the 1950s and 1960s has, however, remained intact in spite of rare exhibitions in England since 1972. His early work has appeared in various exhibitions of St. Ives art and the exhibition of painted sculpture at Francis Graham-Dixon Gallery, London, in 1992, though not successful commercially, elicited respect and interest from an informed audience. This event pointed to a new development in the circumstances of his life - his acquiring a holiday home in the south of France, complete with converted barn studio. This has allowed work to be made once again in Europe, paving the way for exhibitions in British, French or other European galleries.

Wall's sculptural intentions at the end of the 1960s were made explicit in an interview with 'Sculpture International' in October 1969. [12] A key to his success both as a teacher and sculptor was a moral belief in the primacy of personal and individual impulse over acquired attitudes derived from style, fashion and influence. The immediate visual impact of Wall's sculpture is based on the immediacy of welding and on simple clear forms that are neither austerely reductive or elaborately decorative. The works are powerful but discrete entities, well crafted objects true to material and process. Wall has never engaged in the 'roccoco' confections of Caro's late work. Wall's habit of working on several sculptures at once, experimenting with form or transplanting shapes from one piece to another, has at its core an open-ended approach capable of eliciting startling variety and novelty from a limited repertoire. A growing condensation of experience accompanied the making of three dimensional structures without fuss or frill. Despite the move to America, and the harbouring of gigantic ambitions the fundamental language remained the same.

The open-air group exhibitions to which he contributed through-out this period - such as a Scottish Arts Council tour in 1969 and a Holland Park Sculpture Exhibition the following year - certainly encouraged larger scale. But in the last two significant gallery exhibitions before the move to America - the I.C.A's 'British Sculpture Out of the Sixties' and the Royal Academy's 'British Sculptors '72' - Wall's confidence in larger scale was evinced in indoor, rather than outdoor, settings. The former exhibition, selected by the American critic Gene Baro, included 16 younger sculptors whose reputations had been formed during the 1960s and whose work reflected the new possibilities thrown up by that experimental.

While Wall's sculpture of the 1960s was naturally accommodated in such group surveys of British sculpture, sharing an ethos, if not a style, with many of his contemporaries, no other artist worked so exclusively with a restricted range of angled plate, tube and offcut. British sculpture of the 1960s was a hybrid animal: if it looked to America then it did so with a British accent. Equally, when looking to Europe it did so by vernacularising the pure forms and constructive rationality of continental abstraction. Jasia Reichardt introduced British art to an Australian audience in 1967 by stating that 'the basis of art activity in England today... can be realised in any form, with any subject and in any media.' '13 Reichardt's description was of a contemporary British pluralism. Within that pluralism Wall's work stood firm for a judicious balance between improvised expressiveness and constructive purpose. Rather than herald American influence *Cal IV* (1970) and *Long Way* (1971), two large sculptures from the late English period actually employed a grander scale than would characterise much of his subsequent American work.

Gene Baro pointed to a conceptual, intellectual and demonstrative intention at the basis of contemporary British sculpture. Baro's claim that a 'concern with mass seems gradually to have given way to concern with contour and skin' certainly held to Wall's pair of sculptures, *Broken White* (1965) and *Cal IV* in 'British Sculpture out of the Sixties'. Both pieces were complex, disembodied entities extending across space. *Broken White* had already enjoyed considerable exposure in several previous exhibitions. Although Charles Spencer argued in 1966 that the white sculpture was too close to a Caroesque idiom of low-lying dispersed sculpture and possessed 'none of the finality of Wall's best work,' '14 it nevertheless seemed to epitomise the character attributed to sixties sculpture by Baro. The American critic wrote that Wall's pieces 'have the graphic intensity of printed forms,' not in the sense of literally resembling alphabetical or numerical shapes but in the general sense of possessing the vivid, abbreviated, signal-like character of bold typographic design. Sculptures like *Curved III*

Brian Wall (centre) with the author (left) and Denis Bowen at Belgrave Gallery, London. June 2000.

(1969), *Four Circles* (1968) and *Short Hop* (1969), possessed this quality. And later pieces like the appropriately named *Hokus* (1994), *Rollins* (1996) and *Pass* (1997) contain the unmistakeable graphic profiles of a heavily inscribed, leaden calligraphy.

Since retiring from teaching Wall has returned to sculpture-making - and to golf! - with renewed enthusiasm and drive. Alternating between a studio in Oakland, California and one near Montpelier in the south of France, Wall continues to produce convincing new sculpture. An impressive body of new work from Oakland was displayed at the Simon Lowinsky Gallery, New York, in March 1998. In June 1999 recent products from his French studio - an impressive body of low lying horizontal sculptures destined for the floor, were exhibited at Flowers East, London.

FOOTNOTES.

1. Conversation with the author. Beziers, France. Sept. 1997.
2. Henry Abercrombie in conversation with the author. London 4/12/97.
3. Norbert Lynton.
4. Conversation with the author. Sept. 1997.
5. Norbert Lynton. 'Art International.' Sept. l965.
6. Andreae. 30/11/66.
7. John Russell. 'Art News' summer 1966.
8. Norbert Lynton. 'Art International'. Sept. 1965.
9. Edwin Mullins. 'Sunday Telegraph'. 17/4/66.
10. Kenneth Coutts-Smith. 'Lines of Influence'. p.51. 'Art and Artists'. Sept 1968.
11. R.C. Kennedy. 'Art International' Dec. 1968.
12. G.S. Whittet. 'Sculpture International.' Vol 3. No.1. October 1969
13. Jasia Reichardt. Catalogue Introduction to Australian touring exhibition, 'Aspects of New British Art.' 1967.
14. Charles Spencer. 'Sculpture of Simplicity'. 'Studio International'. March 1966.

9

Keith Leonard:
The Search for Essence

Keith Leonard, who was born in Birmingham in 1921 and studied sculpture at the Slade School between 1949 and 1952, was a modest, even self effacing man whose reputation has suffered partly due to his shy temperament and partly to his relatively thin output of sculpture. The sculptures, paintings and numerous drawings he leaves behind are, however, invariably of a high quality, expressing in a pure way the visual ideas that motivated his creativity as an artist. He saw no conflict between the modernity of his artistic project and conventional religion. Like Mondrian, Kandinsky and other modern artists he used the pure language of abstraction to express religious feeling and spiritual truth. Leonard's religious convictions were accompanied by a commitment to teaching and to raising a family, factors that served to place the practise of sculpture in a subordinate role.

Among the sculptors who worked in Barbara Hepworth's St. Ives studio during the 1950s - Leonard worked there on a part time basis between 1955 and 1959 - he was the most highly trained in an academic sense. Under the tutelage of Professor Alfred Gerard, Leonard learnt at the Slade to model the figure or head in a classical way, aware of anatomic proportion and of the balance between mass and space. The figure remained an implicit theme even in the more or less abstract works of the late period, among which *Monument to Pavlova* (1992) distilled the bodily stretches and gyrating movements of dance in general, and ballet in particular, in terms of curved planes twisting around a central axis.

Although never ideologically driven, Leonard was interested in geometry - particularly in lines and straight or curved planes functioning as a complete and perfect expression of poise, balance and tension between static and dynamic forces. The simplified

Keith Leonard
Monument to Pavlova (1992). Fibreglass.

forms of abstract art may have jettisoned descriptive references to nature but movement, direction, weight and scale could be effectively expressed. An early sculpture *Spatial Form* (1953) played visual tricks with perspective, a rectangular plane inserted inside a concave oval tapering inwards to a simulated vanishing point. During this period Leonard studied drawing at the Grande Chaumiére under the sculptor Ossip Zadkine, where he learnt something about sculpture production. Zadkine's predilection towards cubism and allegory did not interest Leonard, whose work inclined towards simplification and minimal, rather than symbolic, abstraction. Drawing under the eye of a prominent 'Ecole de Paris' sculptor did, however, offer the ideal way to fill the gap between leaving the Slade and taking up employment in Hepworth's St. Ives studio.

A pair of contemporaneous plaster sculptures, *Lady* and *Man and Lady* (1953) retained figurative associations in spite of their articulation in post-cubist planes. Their titles reveal pre-occupation with the mystery of sex and gender, though any intention to symbolise sexual difference - hard for male or soft for female, for example, - is subsumed in *Man and Lady* in terms of a monolithic composite. Perhaps one of the most satisfying works of Leonard's small sculptural 'oeuvre', *Man and Lady* is a compressed hybrid of interlocking planes and flat, though bending surfaces. A polished bronze was cast from the original plaster in the 1980s. The enclosed movement of *Man and Lady* did not pertain to another sculpture sharing the theme of gender, *Masculine and Feminine* (1958), which is a lean, open oak carving whose two forms stand on tall stilt-like legs.

Keith Leonard *Masculine and Feminine* (1958). Wood.

The thematic and formal probity of these early sculptures was not, in itself, enough to challenge the situation pertaining throughout his spell working for Hepworth, namely that Leonard's most powerful and defining statements were made on a flat surface. Indeed, Ben Nicholson, by now divorced from Hepworth, wrote to the critic Herbert Read recommending Leonard's drawings which, he told Read, both he and Hepworth 'couldn't resist' [1]. However, a number of large paintings were the most compelling items to emerge during the second half of the 1950s. One of the largest *Burning Bush* (1956) was exhibited in an exhibition called 'Religious Theme' at the Tate Gallery in 1958. Though the image of a burning bush - replete with old Testament associations - is incidentally suggested in the dense stack of criss-crossing, diagonal paint lines, the language of intersection and syncopation is a formal one derived in whole or part from Mondrian. The network of broken lines, while evoking shallow rather than deep space, conjures multi-directional sensations through linear slants and directional rhythms. The principles propounded in Kandinsky's 'Point and Line to a Plane' and in Mondrian's 'Plastic and Pure Plastic Art' are undoubtably reflected in Leonard's paintings.

The Burning Bush was succeeded by the slightly smaller Evening Star Bush (1957), in which a stack of short lines of more or less even length create an oval 'nest' within an off-square horizontal format. Possible cosmological readings are elicited, particularly in And the Little Hills Skipped like Lambs (1957), a centrifugal series of colour waves bursting from a white stellar-like core. Celestial associations are also evoked in another 1957 composition, Sky Forms. A series of straight painted lines fan up and out from an imagined centre below the bottom edge of the picture. Shorn of naturalistic imagery the uncompromising linear energy of Sky Forms creates both neo-religious metaphor and the diagrammatic precision of a mathematic model.

While spatial illusionism is similarly conveyed by modulated lines and planes in Affection (1957), the composition is primarily a carefully considered surface design. This formal reading is enhanced by a restricted palette of white, black and blue. Within the vertical format the deployed shapes are in a balance between vertical and horizontal orientations. A possible interpretation of man-made structures rising out of, or reflected in, surrounding water creates a possible iconographic link with Mondrian's 'pier and ocean' series. Whatever arthistorical model we may find for it, Affection creates rich visual sensation out of a restricted, if directionally varied, vocabulary of truncated lines and planes.

Leonard's participation in the Tate Gallery's 'Religious Theme' exhibition was complemented by a one man show at the Drian Gallery in 1958, an event that confirmed the contemporary relevance of the work. Wall, Leigh and Mitchell, among his St. Ives contemporaries, also exhibited at Halima Nalecz's lively central London gallery. In 1959 a further success saw his installing as head of sculpture at Sunderland School of Art. He held this position until 1962. By 1964 he moved back south to take up a similar position at Farnham School of Art. The conclusion to this successful phase of his career came in 1964 when he exhibited his largest painting The Morning Stars Sang Together at the New York World Fair.

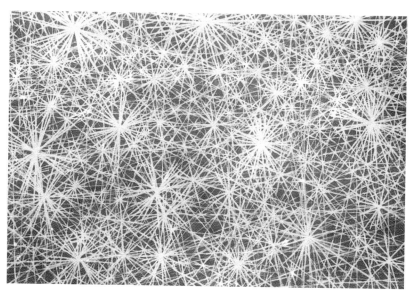

Keith Leonard The Morning Stars Sang Together (1964). Oil on board.

The abstract language of this large blue and white composition followed its predecessors in representing a Christian Scientific convergence between religious metaphor and cosmological exactitude. The blue ground is covered with a constellation of white nodal points. As well as creating a gossamer-like surface texture, the interlinking lines join the scattered points into a family-like assembly. This assembly not only suggests the unified intelligence behind the apparent diversity of creation but also fulfills the modernist criterion of creating a coherent all-over surface capable of being read as an integrated design.

Leonard's later work represents a return to the human dimension of the figure. One of the motives of this later sculpture is the expression of essential physical rhythms perceived in dance.

A number of Leonard's sculptures, in various materials, amounted to distilled expressions of animated figurative posture. The continually turning surfaces of *Youth* (1968), for example, combined several viewpoints of a moving figure within a simplified wood monolith. While teaching at the South Bank Polytechnic, London, in the 1970s Leonard encouraged his students to take an active interest in the sculptural dimension of dance, and even made them use their own bodies to feel such possibilities from within themselves. Extruding limbs and gyrating movements notwithstanding, Leonard kept their attention - and his own - on a traditional notion of the sculpture as a static form. Such experiments, moreover, were therapeutic and empirical in intention and were not conceptual in the sense of leading towards iconic disintegration or towards performance art and 'sculpture-as-body' modes of expression. There was a palpable and refreshing outcome to expressing one's body through space and, in terms of plastic art, would lead to an enhanced feeling for space and the way that sculptural material inhabited and enclosed that space. In Leonard's teaching methods at this juncture we see the St. Ives modernist at play, using the body as a physical vehicle for a greater plastic appreciation of form and of form's relationship to space.

It is not therefore surprising that, upon retiring from teaching, Leonard returned to his St. Ives roots in 1984. As in the case of many distinguished teaching careers, Leonard had tired of the bureaucratic pressures within art school departments, pressures that frustrated not only the direct involvement with students but also the desire to get on with one's own work. The return to St. Ives led inevitably to an improved output of work. The sculpture produced during his final decade in Cornwall soften the hard geometry and clinical precision of modular sculpture made in synthetic materials during the late 1970s. *Multiple Perspex Units* and the more domestic *Small Sculptural Units* (1978) encourage spectator participation (in the rearrangement of 'building block' units) and combine the lightheartedness of toys with the more serious function of the architectural model. The perfect symmetry of these works, though a passing phase, did however inform an outdoor piece, the pristine fibreglass form *Reclining Youth* (1992).

During the course of the early 1980s, it may be fair to say, Leonard continued, as it were, to animate static monolithic forms

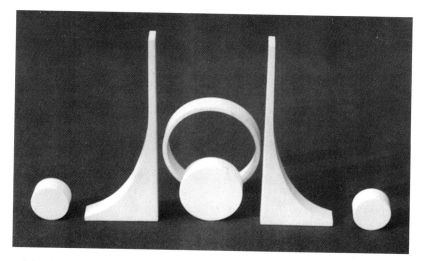

Keith Leonard
*Multiple Perspex
Units* (1978).
Perspex.

with the electricity of lively movement. The pair of upright, forked forms that define the yew carving *Crucifixion* (1980) evoke both the architecture of a cross and the taut musculature and stretched limbs of the body pinned to it. Another wood carving, produced 12 years later, *Calvary* (1992), continues this religious theme but expands the formal content from two to three uprights, the second and third like halved vertical sections of the first. Leonard's religious temperament was tranquil and meditational and this, combined with the underlying formalism of his work, ensured that sculptures like *Crucifixion* and *Calvary* carried none of the expressionistic or overtly emotional dramatics of gothic religious art.

In common with these wood carvings Leonard's last bronzes, *Messenger* (1989) and *Young Woman* (1992), succeed in investing upright planes with the suggestion of movement. Subtle changes of surface are registered by reflected distortion in the polished material. These are slim, stylised sculptures, still bearing titles that reflect the artist's religious instincts. Leonard was adept with many materials and wood continued to offer an appropriate means with which to realise ideas. The idea of constructing wholes from many parts, seen in the modular perspex pieces, also inspired late wood maquettes and small sculptures. These were made from small wood segments, linear and planar in nature, that were glued or bound together in accordion-like expanding or contracting sequences.

Though small in scale one can imagine these intriguing conceptions on a grander, outdoor scale. Leonard certainly embraced the outdoors as an environment for larger sculpture. *Reclining Youth* is interesting for the way its synthetic material looks at home within a landscape setting like Porthmeor beach, St. Ives. Placed on the sand, the sculpture resembled a moored fibreglass boat though its pointed and curved undulation echo wave patterns and tidal rhythms. The form of this sculpture, like its colour, is stripped to structural and aesthetic essentials. Beyond this simplification lies a deeper symbolic purpose, that of expressing the fundamental rhythm of life. The light material of fibreglass also proved an appropriate feature of *Pavlova* (1992), a more complex planar composition which, in common with *Reclining Youth*, was considered to convey 'essences rather than

recognisable human forms.' [2] The critic Christopher Andreae also described it as 'a highly intuitive, three-dimensional 'graph' of a dancer... an image of extraordinarily fastidious sensitivity.' [3] Its description as a 'graph' suggests the plotting and joining of points across space, a process of mathematic precision that is as relevant to Leonards' neo-constructivist means as to thematic content, announced in *And the Morning Stars Sang Together*, about linking disparate points across space. Scientific process thereby joins Christian metaphor in the expression of unity within the apparent diversity of nature.

Keith Leonard
Reclining Youth
(1992). Fibreglass.

The curved, twisting planes of *Pavlova* create a plastic equivalent of a dancing figure. It was displayed in a group exhibition of artists from Cornwall at the Royal West of England Academy, Bristol, in 1992. Its inclusion celebrated Leonard's reclaimed status as a St. Ives artist, but was scant consolation for the artist's conspicuous absence from the large exhibition 'St. Ives 1939-75' held at the Tate Gallery, London in February 1985. The organiser of that exhibition, David Brown, wrote a note for Leonard's memorial exhibition held at the Penwith Galleries, St. Ives, in December 1994. He wrote, 'In the art world the public often accepts at face value the reputations of artists who blow their own trumpets and acquire an undeserved fame. Keith Leonard was a very modest man and suffered as a result. He was unjustly not shown in the 1985 London Tate show.' [4]

Leonard died in December 1993. Since his death a large quantity of high quality drawing and painting on paper has been discovered which reveals an artist brimful of visual ideas that could have been made concrete in terms of further three dimensional work.

Leonard's preoccupation with the theme of dance, particularly ballet, reflected an idealistic sensibility that sought perfection in human terms. This neo-platonic idealism, while opposed to decadence or the overly sensual, was never puritanical. These ideals were never doctrinaire and did not result in a rigid symmetry in his two or three dimensional work. An admiration for the pure language of science meant that measurement and proportion were a means and not an end in themselves. Proportional or numerical systems like the Golden Means or the Fibonacci series heightened an intellectual fascination for structure and stability, but as far as the creation of graphic or sculptural form was concerned he used, not compass or set square, but what felt right to the naked eye.

The St. Ives milieu to which Leonard belonged drew on a palpable post-war mood of optimism and philosophical idealism. Whatever forms such a mood took, the vanguard status of St. Ives had waned by the 1960s and beyond. Leonard, closely associated with Cornish art of the 1950s, was disillusioned with the direction that modern art seemed to take from the early 1960s onward, a direction that saw the pure doctrines of Leonard's generation sullied by the aesthetics of the commercial designer and the ad man. However certain Leonard was concerning artistic values he was always plagued by self doubt and lacked confidence. The tentativeness that resides not only in the volume of work but in its quietism can be seen clearly in the modular sculptures that ask for audience intervention.

Leonard's confidence in the validity of an ongoing artistic project was clearly helped by his marriage to another artist, the painter Charmian Leonard. The marriage to a part Greek, part English painter, led to many trips to Greece, where Charmian's family owned a house on the Aegean island of Poros. The classical architecture and dry landscape of Greece inspired Leonard. The balance and strength of Doric and Ionian temples appealed to both his sense of form and to his religious or mystical inclinations. In particular, Leonard studied at first hand temples like the Parthenon, the Aphia on the island of Aegina and Cape Sounion. In common with Barbara Hepworth, who made visits to Greece in the 1950s, Leonard extracted from the symmetry and constructional purpose of antique architecture lessons that were of relevance to later work.

Like the sculpture, Leonard's abstract drawings never lose touch with nature. Architecture, plants, landscape and the human figure were subjects that moved him to make graphic statements. The drawings were seldom descriptive in a conventional sense. Instead he created linear metaphors of growth or of formal disposition in space. In seeking to express movement or rhythm, Leonard's line seldom became aggressive or heavy. In a series of watercolours, perhaps numbering two dozen, produced during the second half of the 1970s and inspired by his garden at Chertsey, Surrey, Leonard reached a decorative ease recalling Matisse. The series uses the motif of leaves, grouped and suspended in space like the forms of a Calder mobile. The leaves are articulated in pale, thin washes and frequently have no outline, and certainly no structural context like stem or branch. Once again Leonard uses a common natural form to create a metaphor of lightness and repose, the 'calme' if not the 'luxe' or 'volupte' of Matisse's art.

A similar reductive tendency is apparent in several oil paintings composed with a restricted palette of white on white. The shapes, too, are minimal, using ovals and soft edged circles in place of the Russian Suprematist painter Malevich's famous squares. In common with so-called minimal artists like the American painters Robert Ryman and Agnes Martin, Leonard's white paintings contain subtle variations of tone and texture, investing his works with the physical dimension of Ryman and the transcendental illusionism of Martin. The source for Leonard's *In Memory of Jane Nicholson*, however, is specific and biographical, in the sense of its paying tribute to a close friend, the wife of Jake Nicholson. The Leonard family were close friends of Jake and Andrew, offspring of Winifred Dacre's marriage to Ben Nicholson. During a visit to Winifred's family home at Bankshead, Cumbria, Leonard made drawings, schematic rather than descriptive, based on the distinct profiles of Cumbrian hills.

Leonard's graphic work is quintessentially that of a sculptor both for the way its well constructed designs hold the surface of the sheet and stand out in implied space. There is another sense in which Leonard's drawings and paintings are peculiarly the product of a sculptor, and that is to do with an achieved textural dimension. The working of charcoal, paint, graphite or other graphic substances across the paper sheet or canvas weave often deposits rubbed or striated textures redolent of the granular surfaces of wood or stone. This aspect of Leonard's work adds an important dimension to his 'oeuvre' not least for the way it augments the paucity of sculptural output.

FOOTNOTES.

1. Ben Nicholson letter to Herbert Read. c.1956. Courtesy Tate Gallery archive. See also Keith Leonard retrospective catalogue, Penwith Galleries, St. Ives. 1994.
2. Christopher Andreae. 'The Christian Science Monitor' 18/11/93. See also Penwith catalogue 1994.
3. ibid.
4. David Brown. 'Reputations in the World of Art.' Penwith catalogue 1994.

10

A Fusion of Intentions

One of the defining characteristics of St. Ives modernism - a fertile, interdisciplinary overlap between differing branches of the plastic arts - led to a fusion of aesthetic intentions between painting, ceramics, textiles, furniture-making and sculpture. Sound craftsmanship was an achieved virtue linking all areas of the fine and applied arts. The formalist criterion of modern art by no means precluded the human touch; the hand-made quality of many Bauhaus objects formed a precedent and a call to exquisite personal standards of production which also became a noticeable feature of the arts and crafts of St. Ives.

Breon O'Casey who, at the time of writing, has been a Cornish based artist for over 40 years, typifies the emphasis on craft in south-west Cornwall. A painter, printmaker, weaver, jewellery-maker and, latterly, sculptor, O'Casey's vision is closely tied to the physical act of making things for both functional and aesthetic reasons. While the success and integrity of his output is based on honouring the technical means proper to each of the many individual crafts he has tackled, there are nonetheless many instances of fruitful osmosis between them, as for example between painting and weaving or between sculpture and jewellery-making.

O'Casey was born in London in 1928, son of the celebrated Irish playwright Sean O'Casey. In 1937, aged 9, Breon moved with his family to Dartington Hall, near Totnes in Devon where a youngster's raw interest in the arts was encouraged. Dartington became an oasis throughout the war years, building up in the boy enough confidence to pursue studies in London after it. He went on to the Anglo-French Arts Centre in London where the Dartington legacy - later on identified as enabling him to 'think with my hands as well as my head' [1] was complemented by absorption into a broad cosmopolitan culture. It was not, however, until well after this that O'Casey found his artistic feet. What he described as the 'dark', floundering years of the 1950s were followed, at the end of the decade, by his exhilarating discovery of, and successful entry into, the artist's colony of St. Ives. O'Casey's west country roots were thereby consolidated. His modest, quiet temperament made it easy for him to gain friends within this competitive, if close knit, milieu. Another widely-liked man, Denis Mitchell, proved to be the principal social conduit, providing many useful contacts for a developing craftsman and artist.

It was, in fact, through helping out in Mitchell's studio that O'Casey went on to work for Barbara Hepworth. A 'tough apprenticeship' [2] at the hands of the supreme 'taskmaster' ensued. O'Casey, who worked for Hepworth between 1959 and 1962, could not drum up much personal affection for her, though as a professional lesson in the use of tools and materials it was an invaluable experience. The Irish critic Brian Fallon, author of a 1999 monograph on O'Casey, described the legacy of Hepworth as residing in O'Casey's 'care and patience for materials, the spare, often unconventionally elegant forms he uses, the fine but not overfine finish, and an organic unfussy quality.' [3] O'Casey's years working two days a week for Hepworth were a 'sheer economic necessity'; money and an artistic education made him doubly grateful. He fitted in particularly well, O'Casey later writing that he had been asked 'to come for a week, and I think had I been no good that would have been that... she asked me to stay for 3 weeks and then no more was said till I left years later.' [4]

By the time he finally left Hepworth, O'Casey had fully established himself as a St. Ives artist craftsman. From 1959 he exhibited regularly at the Penwith Gallery, becoming vice-Chairman of the Penwith Society during the early 1960s. He also exhibited periodically in London, an early three-man show at Gimpel Fils in 1952 setting an important precedent. During the 1960s he exhibited in the capital several times, notably at the Signals Gallery (1966) and at the Marjorie Parr Gallery. His first show with Parr, in 1967, was shared with Denis Mitchell who, two years later, wrote the catalogue for O'Casey's display of recent paintings and gouaches at the same Chelsea gallery. Mitchell's endorsement of his colleague's work centred on the unostentatious time-honoured craftsmanship common to both. Indeed, Mitchell's identification of the importance of time and patience in the development of his friend's painted images had its source in Mitchell's awareness of the sweat and toil of O'Casey's apprenticeship years. The result, Mitchell concluded, was that O'Casey's pictures 'only reveal their great depth and lyrical qualities after a long time of intimate familiarity.' [5]

The association with Parr was appropriate. Her roots as a dealer lay, not in fine art but in the furniture and glass trade, a factor that predisposed her to take a wide view of arts and crafts in general and of the intimate accord between the fine and applied arts in particular. Profiling her gallery in 1970, the critic Max Wykes Joyce wrote that Parr felt 'very strongly that good ceramics are a particularly excellent form of modern sculpture.' [6] The truth of this was exemplified in the way that Hans Coper's spade forms owed a debt to Brancusi and in the way that younger studio ceramicists like Alison Britton, Ewen Henderson, John Maltby, Peter Hayes and Bernard Irwin, to name but a few, created glazed forms closer to modern sculpture than to traditional pottery. While the production of ceramics is one activity to have eluded him, O'Casey's versatility with many different materials and processes made him an eminently suitable gallery artist for Marjorie Parr.

O'Casey's Cornish roots also proved congenial for a gallery which would, in the spring of 1969, extend its London base by opening a branch in St. Ives. While the St. Ives gallery only lasted until 1973 the same premises later became the Wills Lane Gallery, run first by Reg Singh then by the retired St. Ives architect H.C. Gilbert, the latter displaying O'Casey's work as recently as 2000.

Top: Peter Ward. *Huer*. 1999.

Bottom: Peter Thursby. *Looking Forward*. 1977. Guildhall Square, Exeter.

Brian Fallon's estimation of O'Casey as 'primarily a painter' does not therefore diminish the importance of other facets of his creative output. Were we, however, to order the artist's manifold productions into some kind of creative hierarchy we would inevitably see jewellery-making as a case of economic expediency. That this activity was commercially-driven is suggested both by the abandonment of that craft in the mid 1990s to make way for the new enterprise of sculpture and by a valedictory exhibition in Oxford in 1996 called 'The Last Jewellery Show'. O'Casey's sculpture, however, utilised many ideas explored in silver or gold earrings, in cut-out brooches and in stone and metal necklaces. The sculptures, based on animal, bird or human motifs, divide into solid bronzes and trinket-like silver objects, such as *Feeding Bird* (2000), light and whimsical in quality and using the flat, cut-out shapes of the jewellery.

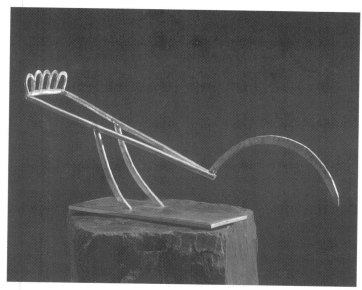

Breon O'Casey
Feeding Bird (2000).
Silver.

O'Casey's approach to painting, in contrast to that of his friend Patrick Heron, is non-intellectual and non-doctrinaire. While colour of a smouldering intensity lends a specific mood and sombre grandeur to the pictures, there is no intention, as there is with Heron, to use the optical properties of pure, unmixed colour to create primary structure. Shape is a positive rather than subordinate element. O'Casey and Heron are, though, similarly inspired by the private cocoon of their respective gardens. The garden provides many artists since Monet with a soothing, yet visually arresting, subject. The link with Monet notwithstanding, O'Casey declares that 'my main influences have been Picasso, Matisse and Braque; and the French school generally. With jewellery Calder, with sculpture perhaps what's called ethnic sculpture'. [7] A redolent primitivism therefore pertains to O'Casey's free-standing forms. *Fish* (1999), an editioned bronze, is a taut, streamlined object mounted on a conic base that is part of the sculptural syntax. Like Brancusi's 1926 prototype O'Casey's *Fish* captures what the Romanian called 'the flash of its spirit'.

The successful outcome of O'Casey's career, based on determination and command of craft, was undoubtedly first learnt during his early years in Hepworth's studio. He described working for her as 'a far stricter training than one gets at art school. You also had to watch your P's and Q's, therefore much more valuable than art school.' [8] While O'Casey remembered their relationship as 'always slightly stiff' a mutual respect ensured a continuance of their professional association. Hepworth bought an O'Casey painting. He made spoons and jewellery to order and, most notably, produced a gold cross for her which, O'Casey remembers, 'she kept mounted on a plastic stand on her mantelpiece.' [9] O'Casey's decision to leave her employment in 1963 was made possible by a part-time post teaching craft at a secondary school in Camborne. This was a timely interception in that both parties had fulfilled their purpose for one another and, as O'Casey later confirmed, by the mid 1960s 'Barbara preferred non-artists as her assistants.' [10]

The increasing professional demands on Hepworth during this period indeed required the recruitment of assistants who were skilled craftsmen in an artisanal, rather than creative, sense. The later Trewyn assistants were willing servants, pleased to undertake tasks of a sometimes mundane and perfunctory kind, who were not sidetracked by separate professional concerns and endeavours. Even as young artists at the outset of their careers the half dozen or so sculptors who assisted during the 1950s had artistic agendas that increasingly impinged on the rigours of the Hepworth enterprise. These agendas saw them distinguish themselves in teaching careers during the 1960s and beyond or expand their output to the extent of needing to employ their own studio assistants. Brian Wall and Keith Leonard became heads of sculpture departments while Mitchell, Milne and O'Casey took on assistants. O'Casey took on the painter and jewellery-maker Brian Illsley as a partner in his jewellery enterprise. John Milne employed Allan Dunn, Colin Hadley, Dirk Rayner and Tommy Rowe.

Hepworth referred to her later assistants as 'the men' (only one woman, Angela Conner, is recorded as having officially worked for her), and they proved loyal and devoted servants. Denis Mitchell, her long-serving stalwart of the 1950s, gave way to a succession of shorter or longer-term workers. Tom Pierce worked there between 1959 and 61; Michael Broido, together with Breon O'Casey assisted between 1959 and 1962. Longer serving assistants like Dicon Nance (1959-71), George Wilkinson (1964-75) and Norman Stocker (1962-75) proved especially useful in Hepworth's twilight years, when physical infirmity required the intervention of trusted craftsmen. Tommy Rowe worked for Hepworth on a part time basis between 1958 and 1962 and, upon completing studies in sculpture and fine art at Bath Academy, Corsham, worked full-time between 1962 and 1964.

Two of the longer-serving helpers, George Wilkinson and Dicon Nance, were Cornish by adoption and birth respectively. Born in Kent in 1920, Wilkinson moved to St. Ives during the war, his marriage to a local girl in 1943 ensuring a lifetime involvement with the town. It was not, however, until the mid 1960s that he began working for Hepworth. Wilkinson subsequently became, in the appreciative words of Hepworth's executor and son-in-law, Sir Alan Bowness, 'an indispensable member of her team.' Bowness alluded to Wilkinson's dedication by stating that the assistant 'had no artistic ambitions. He was simply a willing and wonderful craftsman who learnt quickly and would turn his hand to anything... everything was done with infectious cheerfulness.' [11] Wilkinson's service at Trewyn even extended beyond Hepworth's lifetime. When Trewyn studio was

Barbara Hepworth's 70th birthday party, Tregenna Castle Hotel, St. Ives, 10th January 1973. Brian Smith (left), Tate Gallery Trustee Anthony Lousada (far left), guitarist John Williams (far right) were present. In the background are Mrs. Breon O'Casey, the Scott-Browns and Penwith Secretary Kathy Watkins (far right).

opened as a museum the year after Hepworth's death, he helped curator Brian Smith and Jacqui Watson run the enterprise, maintaining the fabric of the building. He also helped the upkeep of its semi-exotic garden both until the Museum was taken over by the Tate Gallery in 1980 and during the succeeding years leading to his retirement in 1986.

Wilkinson's perceived lack of 'artistic ambitions' place him firmly on one side of the putative divide between craft and fine art. Such a divide had an acrimonious history in the competitive climate of post war St. Ives art. The Penwith Society's distinction between fine art and craft had, after all, caused much trouble shortly after its founding in 1949. The technical and aesthetic concerns of painters, sculptors, potters, furniture-makers and others frequently overlapped in a way that blurred the distinctions between the various branches of the plastic arts. Dicon Nance, son of the Cornish painter Robert Morton Nance, saw this situation from the viewpoint of the craftsman and the artist. He stood for high technical standards and adopted an abrasive attitude to what he sometimes saw as sloppiness in the work of potters and sculptors alike. During the years he worked for Hepworth, a period that Tanya Harrod described as 'his final disillusion with the art world' [12], Nance also questioned the validity of the artist's role, particularly when the physical execution of her designs fell exclusively on the shoulders of craftsmen such as himself.

Nance entered the Leach pottery in the 1930s, where he maintained machinery. He spent part of the war in Africa, helping the potters Harry Davis and Michael Cardew and here, too, Nance perceived the lofty aesthetics of 'high' art undermined by carelessness in the production of both domestic ware and 'studio' pots. Returning from Africa in 1945, Nance helped his brother Robin, the distinguished furniture-maker, open a workshop on the Wharf at St. Ives in 1946. In much the same way that Leach had done with pottery, the Nance workshop introduced a spare, elegant look favoured by modernism. The picture frames and sculpture bases that the workshop provided for Hepworth drew attention to the

95

handmade quality of even the most clinical or precise forms of modern art.

Norman Stocker's engineering background enabled him to help with Hepworth's larger sculptures and metal structures. He was a general member of the team and helped on Hepworth's marble sculptures. Stocker travelled with Wilkinson and Nance to London during the spring of 1968 to help prepare for her Tate Gallery retrospective.

The case of Tommy Rowe casts further shadow on the dividing line between craft and art. Born locally in 1941, he attended Bath Academy, Corsham from 1959 to l962. Entering Trewyn studio in 1958 as a raw 17 year-old, Rowe was introduced to the working procedures of an internationally renowned sculptor. He later assisted John Milne and Denis Mitchell, forming with the latter a particularly close working relationship that lasted until Mitchell's death. Rowe's fitful production of sculpture of his own did not preclude participation in some group exhibitions at the Marjorie Parr Gallery. While Rowe's employment at Trewyn - part time while a student and full time for a couple of years afterwards - saw him learn to carve wood and slate forms, his course work at art school saw an involvement with the more contemporary mode of minimal and constructed sculpture. Taught by John Hoskin, who no doubt encouraged metal, Rowe welded sheet steel, creating intriguing box-like forms. Something of these simple structures inform subsequent carvings, which were inspired by the experience of seeing cliffs and other impressive coastal outcrops from a fishing vessel. He later relied more and more on fishing for a livelihood, and spent two years during the mid 1960s working in north Wales in forestry. These activities did not, however, prevent the long working partnership with Mitchell. He enjoyed this relationship, based on equality. 'It wasn't so precious... and it wasn't so involved with recognition and fame,' [13] he recalled.

Tommy Rowe *Cliff Forms*. Guarea. 1999.

Rowe's student flirtation with metal and industrial processes became a full-blown marriage in the case of the sculptor, painter and relief-maker Peter Ward. Ward's experience in establishing himself as a sculptor offers marked, and instructive, contrast to that of his younger Cornish contemporary. Born in London in 1932, Ward had precious little formal art training. What he learnt about design came during the years he worked as a pattern maker at Vickers Armstrong in Surrey. During the decade or so employed by the firm Ward took advantage of day release schemes to attend part-time courses at Kingston College of Art. By the early 1960s, however, Ward had left his engineering background and elected to become a full-time artist. He did not enjoy Rowe's advantage of working for Hepworth; during the impecunious few years spent as a struggling St. Ives artist in the early 1960s Ward tried in vain to gain employment in Hepworth's studio.

In common with many modern sculptors Ward began as a painter, later turning to sculpture as a natural extension of the modernist need to let the materials do the talking and allow specific technical processes govern the expressive outcome. Seen in this light it is not surprising that Ward's paintings have a 'sculptural' robustness of composition, aching to be realised in a palpable, tactile dimension, while his sculptures use the graphic language of linear silhouette, collage and decorative treatment of surfaces proper to the pictorial arts. In the case of both a strong feeling for structural pattern betrays a background in industrial design. Many of his paintings, reliefs and free-standing objects employ distinctive curvilinear rhythms and wave-like patterns that are as much a reflection of cutting and shaping hard materials with power tools as of an abiding preference for the iconography of the sea. The captivating rhythm of tidal expansion and contraction is a leitmotif throughout Ward's work in all media, investing his brand of abstraction with a vital current of naturalism.

A seminal painting like the aptly named *Industrial Composition* (1963) contains strong accents of primary colour within an imposing structural grid of straight and curved black lines. These black lines recall the lead of stained glass windows while also positing a strong link with welded steel sculpture. As such the picture invites replication in the third dimension. The much later *Wave Figure* (1995), on the other hand, replicates in terms of an upright carved and constructed Portland stone monolith the pronounced stepped patterns of collaged curvilinear planes which are a feature of cardboard or plastic reliefs. Irrespective of material, therefore, undulating patterns run across the two and three dimensional work of the 1990s, featuring in two differently sized bronze versions of *Wave Figure* (1993 and 1999) as well as in the intervening stone.

The difficulty of raising a family and making a living purely from painting compelled an early return to Surrey, where from 1967 until 1983 he lectured in art and design in Guildford. The years as a senior lecturer at West Surrey College of Art (an amalgam of Guildford and Farnham art colleges) were distinguished by his introducing into new metal courses the rigours of industrial engineering that had been encountered in an aeroplane and motor car factory. With Peter Parkinson he developed the first cold blast cupola for making cast iron objects in a British art school. Ward made several cast iron pots, which integrate the arts and crafts tradition of pottery with the industrial ethos of the new metal technologies. By the early 1980s Ward had finally secured himself financially and in 1983 decided to jack in teaching and fulfil a long standing dream of setting up permanently as a St. Ives-based painter and sculptor. Aged 50 he returned to Cornwall and developed sculpture, particularly in metal, as his primary vehicle of expression.

Ward's concentration on sculpture from the mid 1980s onwards was a timely and salutary interception within an art colony in which an absurd and growing imbalance existed between painting and sculpture. Even in Hepworth's heyday St. Ives sculptors, who form the focus of the present study, were overwhelmingly outnumbered by painters and potters. A major commission *Marine Elements* (1988) for Warsash Marine College in Hampshire proved, in the words of his old colleague John Mitchell, 'the prelude to a decade of sustained sculptural production' [14]. Ward's sculpture appeared to grow in confidence as a result of this commission. The architectonic language of this steel plate wall-bound construction, and its accompanying maquettes in painted marine ply, fulfilled the artist's description of his sculpture being 'a combination of engineering and art' [15]. Iconographically, the imagery of the *Marine Elements* series reflect the objects of West Penwith's industrial scene, in particular anchors and moorings rings. While retaining the 'overtly emblematic' [16] character of *Marine Elements*, many of the bronze, or partly bronze, sculptures of the 1990s reflect less the industrial, than the natural tidal, aspects of Cornwall's coastal landscape. Some, like *Wave Figure* (1993), *Sun Wave* (1994) and *Small Wave* (1999), introduce extraneous materials suggesting a richly allusive or associative dimension. The bronze elements are pinned to black granite or slate bases, which form part of the formal syntax. Since these differing materials are accommodated as part of the structural 'stack' the observer is reminded of Brancusi. Ward owes an even greater debt to this colossus of modern sculpture in *Ascending Ellipses*, an upright zig-zagging arrangement. Closer to home the influence of Denis Mitchell is apparent in *Nancledra* (1999), a simple upright configuration of interlocked planes cast from a wood maquette. In the Mitchell manner it bears a Cornish title.

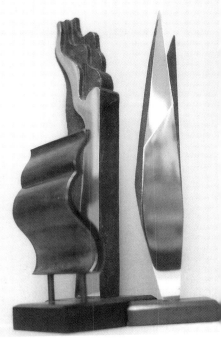

Peter Ward *Wave Figure* (1995) and right *Nancledra* (1999).

The vertical orientation of *Ascending Ellipses* was taken up in a series of slim welded steel 'totems', ten of which were included in Ward's second large exhibition at the Penwith Galleries, St. Ives, during the spring of 2000. These innovations not only mark a new departure but also confirm principles integral to previous work, in particular the predilection for simple, ready-made, geometric components. The offcuts, acquired from Andrews' steel yard in Redruth, are used in simple, but richly varied, combinations. Despite the ancestral - not to mention Hepworthian - associations of these sentinel-like 'figures', Ward's fundamental motive is formal and architectural. Structural logic is integral to the work's aesthetic effect. While eschewing the driftwood romanticism favoured by certain earlier St. Ives artists - such as Peter Lanyon and Margaret Mellis - these industrial, yet delicately poised, ensembles salute the pristine constructivist classicism of early St. Ives modernism. And in deference to the perfectionism of that tradition Ward finishes the four or five steel beams and cylinders that make up pieces like *Huer* (1999) with an even matt black weatherproof paint. The interiors, by contrast, are blood red, an apparent tribute to Terry Frost's Spanish-derived use of black and red.

A degree of skilled engineering is also evident in a series of cardboard and plastic reliefs, the latter produced by a vacuum former. The stepped patterns of these shallow space reliefs simulate such natural phenomena as waves dissolving across wet sand or the ribbed patterns left on the sand by receding tides. Whatever association is made, these reliefs are deft exercises in precision collaging using pre-formed curvilinear sections. Standing half way between painting and sculpture, Ward's reliefs also declare the salient theme of the sea.

A similar engineering background to Ward's is an integral feature of the well constructed metal sculpture of Gordon Allen (b.1925). While Allen served in the navy during and after the war, it was to aeronautical engineering that he later turned. He worked at the Vickers Armstrong aircraft division in Swindon between 1952 and 1978. Unlike Ward, Allen never left Vickers for a post in an art college department, but learnt much about metal and metal engineering during his time at the firm. Allen's knowledge of metals informed the abstract shapes that his sculpture took, spiralling or curving shapes that express the eddying rhythms of air currents. Not only in a technical, but also a conceptual sense the years spent with Vickers therefore had a direct artistic impact.

Gordon Allen *Jacob's Ladder* (1998). Stainless Steel. The sculpture is seen in the Salthouse Gallery, St. Ives.

While a full-time job limited the time available to make sculpture Allen spent much spare time developing as an artist. In 1960 he started making sculpture in plaster and cement and by the 1980s worked successfully in stainless steel. He was an active member of the Swindon Artists Society where he knew Roger Leigh. In 1970 and 71 work was accepted at the Royal West of England Academy, Bristol and at the Royal Academy, London, respectively. His Royal Academy sculpture *Windy Day* was inspired by a whirlwind of dust whipped up by a gust of wind, the fugitive, fleeting effects of nature conjured through the solid and calculated precision of his work. Since moving to St. Ives in 1997 Allen became an associate member of the Penwith Society, displaying elegant steel or aluminium compositions like *Jacob's Ladder*, a seamless upright configuration of metal elements that emulate the decorative humour of cubist construction. At his Carn Brea workshop, near Redruth, Allen has produced a series of sculptures that, in spite of modern technological processes, have a mythic and totemic stance.

These sculptures utilise a stock of light alloys that Allen retrieved from the Concorde project during his Vickers days. *Jacob's Ladder* also incorporates steel scrap that Allen collected from the earlier Spitfire aircraft project. Together these aircraft materials are used anthropomorphically, or in Allen's words, 'to demonstrate the historical shift from ancient times to the present day.' '[17]

The sculpture of Peter Thursby shares the industrial connotations of Ward and Allen. Thursby's art school background - he studied in Bristol and Exeter during the early 1950s - distinguishes him from the engineering backgrounds of Ward and Allen. From an early age Thursby was inspired by the shapes of industrial scrap metal. His west country credentials makes him a St. Ives sculptor by proxy. He exhibited with both the Penwith Society and Newlyn Society during the 1960s and, perhaps more significantly, exhibited alongside Mitchell, Leigh, Milne and O'Casey at the Marjorie Parr Gallery, where he enjoyed three solo exhibitions in 1964, 65 and 1971.

In marked contrast to that of his sculptor contemporaries from St. Ives, however, Thursby's career is highlighted by an extended and successful dialogue with architects. To this extent Thursby sets to one side the random subjectivity, individual vision and hands-on craftsmanship of the traditional sculpture atelier and fulfils the Bauhaus imperative of fine artists collaborating with designers, town planners, engineers or architects in the fabrication of a harmonious environment. In Thursby's able hands form becomes one with content: the sculpture a product of good cerebral design, strong structural logic and sound engineering. Thursby's habit of collaborating with architects or planners, coupled with a formal and thematic interest in vertical structures that symbolise upward movement and natural growth, broadly relates his sculpture to the constructivist tradition. Aware of the vital role played by space alongside that of solid form, Thursby encourages a romantic dialogue with light and, where a series of Fountain sculptures are concerned, with water. The Fountain sculptures, situated in prominent public locations in Exeter, Tunbridge Wells, north London and Dallas, Texas sees water inject an ephemeral dimension to the static monumentality of concrete form. *Looking Forward* (1977) and *High Levels* (1988), fountain sculptures at Exeter and Finchley respectively, have the hieratic presence of giant heads, a possible hint that Thursby's roots lay, not in abstract art, but in the figurative expressionism of the 1950s.

Peter Thursby *High Levels* (1988). Bronze.

The convergence of the aesthetic and functional in these instances does not preclude a visionary impulse; in their thrusting verticality sculptures such as *Tower of Intersecting Planes* aim towards the sky like jets of water. Whatever debt is owed to Tatlin's 'Tower', constructivism's unrealised 'magnum opus', or to Caro's recent 'sculpitecture', there is no doubting the Devon-based sculptor's crucial preoccupation with upward movement. A recent sculpture series *Optimism*, made in bronze or silver and accompanied by many small, medium or large scale studies on paper, pushes abstract form towards naturalistic metaphor. The infinitely complex silhouettes and jagged cut-out profiles created by soldering bronze sheets together makes an almost tangible reference to branches touching the sun or to endlessly moving figures in a crowd. Thursby's sculpture indeed makes us think carefully about the meaning of the word abstract. While the language uses resolute, if asymetric, geometry, the dynamic tension between vertical and horizontal axes deposits a feeling of lively expansion. A sensual feeling for surface, ranging from opaque bronze patinas to the sparkling polish of stainless steel, aluminium or sterling silver, enhances the associative dimension of the work.

The *Optimism* sculptures are the product of stark graphic inventiveness. He also experiments with working models in polystyrene or plaster. Ideas are finally realised through technical assistants in foundries. The lively feeling for profile and silhouette reflects Thursby's roots in painting. Taught at the West of England College of Art, Bristol, by Ernest Pascoe and Paul Feiler, Thursby went on to produce many abstract paintings. By the time of his solo exhibition at the Arnolfini, Bristol in 1963, however, Thursby had established sculpture as his prime mode of expression. The 'architectonic' quality of his work was no doubt encouraged by friendship with Roger Leigh, who for many years lodged once a week at the Thursby's Exeter home while teaching part-time at Exeter College of Art.

Thursby, first sculptor President of the Royal West of England Academy, Bristol (between 1995 and 2000) drove sculpture further up the R.W.A. agenda. He has been aided in this by Ann Christopher R.A. a Wiltshire-based sculptor who trained at Bristol between 1966 and 1969. Christopher's slim, upright forms, in bronze, steel and other durable metals, are broad composites encompassing architecture

Ann Christopher *Cutting Line* (1996). Corten Steel.

and the figure. They reveal sensitivity to plane, line and edge - the former often subtly curved, the latter jagged. These 'primitive' edges mitigate the modern industrial connotations of engineering and construction. Christopher's *Cutting Line* (1996) a site specific corten steel monument located at Marsh Mills, Plymouth, stands both as erect totem and as portal, investing the minimal sheet steel constructions of the American sculptor Richard Serra with an anthropomorphic dimension.

The St. Just-based sculptor Paul Mount (b.1922), in contrast to Leigh, never trained in architecture but always worked with architectural projects. In Nigeria during the 1950s Mount worked on his first architectural projects. Before that point Mount had studied and practised as a painter, another feature he shares with Thursby and indeed with many modern sculptors whose first artistic outpourings were with paint and canvas. To a greater extent than Thursby, however, whose sculptures tend to originate from graphic designs and studies, Mount rehearses and resolves his forms empirically through the fabrication of scale models using card, wax, polystyrene and other flexible and makeshift materials. The nature of these materials influence the final outcome in cast or constructed metals. Card is used in the design of sculptures fabricated with sheets of cut or bent metal; wax or plaster for cast bronzes; polystyrene for unique, un-editioned cast iron sculptures. 'My own inclination,' Mount has written 'is to use materials in their most characteristic way, consistent with ease of working, stability of structure'. [18]

Paul Mount was born and educated in Devon, later studying at the Royal College, London. Spells teaching in Winchester and in west Africa notwithstanding, Mount remained true to his west country origins, working in Cornwall since returning from a seven-year period in Africa in 1962. As a design consultant on building projects in Nigeria, Mount worked with such distinguished architects as the Polish Borys and Fry, Drew and Atkinson. The first three-dimensional structure Mount designed was an extended concrete wall in Ikoyi, Nigeria. Aware from that point that sculpture associated with buildings 'needs to be on a massive scale to be effective,' [19] Mount became conscious of the importance of structural engineering both from a technical and aesthetic viewpoint. The concrete wall also established a penchant for rectilinear movements within multi-part or uniform sculptures. Open or recessive space also played a vital role within the complex configuration, Mount writing in 1985 that a sculptor 'needs to be aware of the space that he creates as much as the solid.' [20]

Paul Mount *Skysails* (1970). Stainless Steel.

Mount's awareness of sculpture as architectural embellishment, informed and inspired by Romanesque bas relief (Mount spent much time visiting Romanesque churches in France and wrote an informed essay on the subject), has led to some successful large scale sculptures in architectural locations. *Spirit of Bristol* (1968) and *SkySails* (1970), both stainless steel constructions originally made for sites in the centre of Bristol, make pertinent references to the theme of sailing, which they evoke through taut or curved forms that are clearly derived from the shapes of boats and sails. The thrusting shapes of *Spirit of Bristol* also contain faint Mariniesque equestrian overtones. Both sculptures exploit the versatile material of stainless steel plate, which is cut, bent and welded. The armada of eight enclosed forms that comprise *SkySails* were inspired by a childhood passion for windjammers, which Mount directly experienced through a sailor grandfather. Originally located at Welshback, Bristol, *SkySails* was relocated in 1999 to Exeter University, where it is attached to a prominent brick building on the campus.

Mount's concerns for sculpture interacting not only with architecture but also with people has led, in certain instances, to the making of loose, multi-part structures. These encourage audience participation in the literal sense of inviting a re-arrangement of interchangeable elements. An extension of this idea led Mount to make mobiles, lighthearted sculptures made from offcuts of stainless steel plate (usually in triangle or rectangle formats) which are attached to thin 'arms' or 'branches'. Inevitable naturalistic overtones ensue from their movement in the wind, a situation evoking rustling leaves in summer breezes.

These romantic overtones temper the impact of hard materials, industrial processes and a language of abstract, geometric form. His love of music, and knowledge of musical structure, is at play not only in the kinetic constructions but also in static bronze figures inspired by the theme of dance. The least sculptural of Mount's three dimensional work, these dancers have a stylised and whimsical quality and as such do not impress as much as a series of solid, compact, interlocked compositions inspired by the monumental power of natural or man-made Cornish rock formations. Mount, a well adjusted, modest artist who has the ideal partner in the painter June Miles, correctly views the cast iron sculpture as his 'most characteristic' work. The distinctive orange and brown rust 'patina', together with pitted surface texture effected from originating polystyrene, imparts an earthy gravity to heavy, unique iron sculptures Nonetheless, erect upright sculptures like *Umbrella Man* (1984), *Fantasia* (1996) and *Oracle* (1997) engage with air, light, space in a lyrical way. The interlocking complexity of curved, straight, horizontal or vertical elements is baroque in spirit. In contrast to the frontal pictoriality of relief sculpture these intricate configurations invite thorough investigation from all sides, their complexity enhanced by highlight and shadow. What the artist has termed a 'sense of precariousness to engender vitality' is an intended feature of the open and closed rhythms of these cast iron works. In later years Mount has sold work to a discriminating Spanish collector, and *Umbrella Man* and *Fantasia*, to name but two, are iron works in a terminal - and highly appropriate - Spanish landscape setting. The English sculptor's work has in fact long been inspired by the Spanish master of forged iron sculpture, Eduardo Chillida (b.1924). Chillida's 'Modulation of Space' series (c.1963) defines and creates space through the deft movements of heavy, lumpen shapes.

The deployment of sculptural form in an open description or encapsulation of space does not, in the case of either Chillida or Mount, amount to a systematic free-standing calligraphy. In contrast to Calder or the sculptor welders like Gonzalez, Smith and Caro, Mount prefers the grounded monument to the illusion of weightless aerodynamic 'writing'. Broadly conforming to an upright square or rectangular 'box', Mount's cast iron, bronze or stainless steel compositions are no more the product of a three-dimensional drawing than their generally vertical format is totemic. Whereas David Smith described even the geometric components of the 'Cubis' as 'found objects' Mount speaks not of 'objets trouvé' but of 'objets fabriqué' - 'bits of my own fabrication cut up from earlier designs' [21]: Recycling and backtracking highlights the open-ended, 'work-in-progress' nature of Mount's endeavour; an empiricism closely aligned with materials and the working of those materials. Mount continues to practice both drawing and painting on flat paper or canvas supports, not as direct plans or rehearsals for work in the round, but as a separate discipline informed by the sensual texture and physical form of sculpture. The separation - even division of labour - between drawing and sculpture further emphasises the direct and unpredictable process of his mode of sculpture-making; structurally and optically stable, Mount's sculptures are also asymetric, achieving the intended 'sense of precariousness to engender vitality.'

FOOTNOTES

1. Breon O'Casey 'Life and Times' .p.47. Scolar Press 1999.
2. Brian Fallon. 'Breon O'Casey' .p.16. Scolar Press 1999.
3. ibid.
4. Letter to the author. Jan 2000.
5. Denis Mitchell. Catalogue note for Breon O'Casey exhibition at Marjorie Parr gallery, London, Oct. 2-25 1969.
6. Max Wykes-Joyce. 'Marjorie Parr'. 'Arts Review'. 14/2/1970.
7. Letter to the author, Jan. 2000.
8. ibid.
9. ibid.
10. ibid.
11. Alan Bowness. 'George Wilkinson'. Obituary for 'St. Ives Times and Echo' 17/4/1998.
12. Tanya Harrod. 'The Crafts in Britain in the Twentieth Century' p.167 Yale University Press 1999.
13. Tommy Rowe in conversation with the author Paul. Cornwall. 21/12/99.
14. John Mitchell. Catalogue Introduction for Peter Ward exhibition at Penwith Galleries, St. Ives. April 1997.
15. Peter Ward.Catalogue note for Penwith exhibition. 1997.
16. Mitchell Penwith Gallery catalogue. 1997.
17. Gordon Allen note to the author. 16/6/2000.
18. Paul Mount. 'A Constructive Approach to Sculpture'. 1985.
19. ibid.
20. ibid.
21. ibid.

List of Black & White Illustrations

Frontispiece: Denis Mitchell in his studio with *Skiddaw* (1974).

1. Denis Mitchell exhibition at Flowers East, London. March 1993.
    Photo courtesy Jane Mitchell.
    Mitchell exhibition. Flowers East. Courtesy Jane Mitchell.
    Denis Mitchell. *Zelah 11*. Courtesy Jane Mitchell.
    Denis Mitchell. *Carn*. 1961.
    Denis Mitchell bronzes. Photo Phillips Auctioneers, London.
    Courtesy James Rawling.
    Denis Mitchell. *Argos*. 1974. Photo courtesy Jane Mitchell.

2. Denis Mitchell, Mary Lambert, Marjorie Parr and Breon O'Casey,
    London early 1970s. Photo courtesy Mary Lambert.
    Tommy Rowe with Denis Mitchell Newlyn early 1970s. Photo
    courtesy Tommy Rowe.
    Denis Mitchell. *Traeve*. 1992. Photo: Pandy Pandelis.
    Denis Mitchell with *Zennor Head*. 1985. Courtesy Tommy Rowe.
    Denis Mitchell. *Gemini*. 1973. Photo courtesy Jane Mitchell.
    Denis Mitchell. *Tresco*. 1984.
    Denis Mitchell at Marjorie Parr Gallery, London, early 1970s. Photo
    courtesy Mary Lambert.

3. John Milne. *Vertical Form*. 1954. Photo courtesy Belgrave Gallery,
    London.
    Constantin Brancusi. 'The Kiss'. 1908. Collection Craiova Museum,
    Romania.
    John Milne. *The Kiss*. 1957. Photo courtesy Stanley Sellers,
    Birmingham.
    Barbara Hepworth. Wood sculpture. Photo courtesy Tommy Rowe.

4. Ivaldo Ferrari outside Marjorie Parr Gallery, St. Ives. Photo courtesy
    Mary Lambert.
    Trewyn House, St. Ives, late 1990s. Photo courtesy Harding Laity,
    St. Ives.
    John Milne at Delphi, Greece, 1960s. Photo: Stanley Sellers.
    John Milne. *Easter Island Form*. 1966. Photo courtesy Belgrave
    Gallery, London.
    John Milne. *Anakalypsis*. 1967. Photo courtesy Belgrave Gallery,
    London.
    John Milne. *Prometheus*. 1967. Photo courtesy Belgrave Gallery.

5. John Milne on Porthmeor with Colin Hadley and Tommy Rowe.
    Photo Belgrave Gallery.
    John Milne. *Persepolis*. 1971. Photo courtesy Belgrave Gallery.
    John Milne. *Atlas 11*. 1974. Photo courtesy Belgrave Gallery.
    John Milne. *Oneiros*. 1973. Photo courtesy Belgrave Gallery.
    John Milne. *Todra*. 1974. Photo courtesy Belgrave Gallery.
    John Milne. *Cybele*. 1974. Collection Giovanni Tieuli.

6. Barbara Hepworth in her garden. Photo courtesy Tommy Rowe.
    Roger Leigh carving 'Hieroglyph'. 1953. Photo courtesy Nicholas
    Leigh.
    Roger Leigh. *Counterthrust*. 1957. Photo courtesy Nicholas Leigh.
    Roger Leigh. *Untitled*. Collection Denis Bowen. Photo courtesy
    Nicholas Leigh.

Roger Leigh. *Flowerhead*. 1965. Photo courtesy Nicholas Leigh.
Roger Leigh. *Diamond Discharge*. 1965. Photo courtesy Nicholas Leigh.
Roger Leigh. *Portico*. 1969. Photo courtesy Nicholas Leigh.
Roger Leigh. *Flatsider*. 1969. Photo courtesy Nicholas Leigh.
Roger Leigh. *Partition*. 1969. Collection University of Exeter. Photo courtesy Nicholas Leigh.
Roger Leigh. *Wind Pivot*. 1971. Photo courtesy Nicholas Leigh.
'Sorbus' Leigh's architect-designed house at Aldbourne, Wilts. Photo courtesy Nicholas Leigh.
Roger Leigh masquerading with a ceramic sculpture. 1990s. Photo courtesy Nicholas Leigh.

7.   Brian Wall on Porthmeor Beach, St. Ives. c.1957. Photo courtesy Brian Smith.
Brian Wall. *Right Angle Deck Construction*. 1956.
Brian Wall. *Sculpture 1956*. Photo courtesy Whitford Fine Art.

8.   Brian Wall. *Long Way*. 1971. Photo: Royal Academy of Arts, London.
Brian Wall. *Upright Figure*. 1962. Collection Whitford Fine Art, London. Photo courtesy Whitford Fine Art.
Brian Wall. *Untitled Black*. 1964. Collection Whitworth Art Gallery, Manchester. Photo courtesy University of Manchester.
Brian Wall. *Untitled*. 1960s.
Robert Adams. 'Figure'. 1950. Photo courtesy René Gimpel, Gimpel Fils, London.
Brian Wall. *Small Construction*. 1962. Collection W.H.R. Cayton, London.
Brian Wall. *Right On*. 1970.
Brian Wall with Denis Bowen and the author, Belgrave Gallery, London. June 2000. Photo Michael Gacca.

9.   Keith Leonard. *Monument to Pavlova*. 1992. Collection Charmian Leonard, Surrey. Photo courtesy Charmian Leonard.
Keith Leonard. *Masculine and Feminine*. 1958. Photo courtesy Charmian Leonard.
Keith Leonard. *The Morning Stars Sang Together*. 1964. Collection Charmian Leonard. Photo courtesy Charmian Leonard.
Keith Leonard. *Multiple Perspex Units*. 1978. Photo courtesy Charmian Leonard.
Keith Leonard. *Reclining Youth*. Collection Charmian Leonard. Photo: Mark Leonard.

10.   Breon O'Casey. *Feeding Bird*. 2000. Photo courtesy Breon O'Casey.
Barbara Hepworth's 70th birthday party, Tregenna Castle Hotel, St. Ives. January 10 1973. Photo Percy Smith. Photo courtesy Brian Smith, St. Ives.
Tommy Rowe. *Cliff Forms*. 1999. Photo courtesy Tommy Rowe.
Peter Ward. *Wave Figure* 1995, and *Nancledra* 1999. Photo courtesy Peter Ward.
Gordon Allen. *Jacobs Ladder* 1998 in the Salthouse Gallery, St. Ives. Photo courtesy Gordon Allen.
Peter Thursby. *High Levels*. 1988. Collection McDonalds Hamburgers. Photo courtesy Peter Thursby.
Ann Christopher. *Cutting Line*. 1996. Photo courtesy Ann Christopher.
Paul Mount. *Skysails*. 1970. Collection University of Exeter. Photo courtesy Paul Mount.

List of Colour Illustrations

Denis Mitchell. *Trewarveneth*. 1992. Collection Glynn Vivian Art Gallery, Swansea. Photo courtesy Glynn Vivian.

Denis Mitchell. *Porthgwarra*. 1961. Collection Belgrave Gallery. Photo courtesy Belgrave Gallery, London.

Denis Mitchell. Collection of bronze sculptures. Photo courtesy Phillips auctioneers, London.

John Milne. *Cylindrical Form*. 1966. Photo Stanley Sellers.

Liam Hanley. 'Ship and Sculptural Form'. Photo courtesy Liam Hanley.

Michael Canney. *Untitled*. 1984. Collection Madeleine Canney. Photo courtesy M. Canney.

Brian Wall. *Sculpture 1956*. Collection Whitford Fine Art, London. Photo courtesy Whitford Fine Art.

Brian Wall. *Upright Figure*. 1962. Collection Whitford Fine Art, London. Photo courtesy Whitford Fine Art.

Keith Leonard. *Male and Female*. Collection W.H.R. Cayton. Photo courtesy W.H.R. Cayton.

Keith Leonard outside his studio. St. Ives. February 1991. Photo courtesy Charmian Leonard.

Roger Leigh. *Solstice*. 1959. Collection Anne Christopherson. Photo Anne Christopherson, London.

Breon O'Casey. *Fish*. 1999. Collection Breon O'Casey. Photo courtesy Breon O'Casey.

Peter Ward. *Huerl*. 1999. Photo courtesy Peter Ward.

Peter Thursby. *Looking Forward*. 1977. Guildhall Square, Exeter. Collection Exeter City Council. Photo courtesy Peter Thursby.

Paul Mount. *Fantasia*. 1997. Photo courtesy Paul Mount.

Breon O'Casey with John Wells. Early 1970s. Photo courtesy Breon O'Casey.

Index

A

Abercrombie, Henry *72*
Adams, Robert *46, 47, 69, 70, 72, 77, 78*
Allen, Gordon *99, 100*
Alloway, Lawrence *64, 70, 72, 77, 78*
Andreae, Christopher *76, 77, 88*
Anton, Victor *69*
Armitage, K. *66*
Arp, Jean *69*
Ascot, Roy *72*
Auricoste, Emmanuel *27*
Ayrton, Michael *66*

B

Ballard, Arthur *53*
Barns-Graham, W. *18, 30*
Baro, Gene *80, 81*
Bell, Trevor *68*
Berlin, Sven *6*
Bill, Max *69*
Bourdelle, *66*
Bowen, Denis *40, 48, 56, 72*
Bowness, Alan *18, 70, 94*
Brancusi, Constantin *11, 23, 24, 27, 29, 30, 33, 34, 35, 39, 49, 66, 92, 93, 98*
Braque, Georges *93*
Brennan, Robert *64*
Britton, Alison *92*
Broido, Michael *94*
Brooker, William *72*
Brown, David *7, 88*
Brown, Sylvia *80*

C

Calder, Alexander *89, 93, 103*
Canney, Michael *61, 62, 69*
Cardew, Michael *95*
Caro, Anthony *72, 73, 74, 76, 77, 79, 80, 100, 103*
Carver, T. *4, 6*
Cézar, *66*
Chadwick, Lynn *40, 66*
Chillida, Eduardo *62, 103*
Christopher, Ann *101*
Coates, Wells *43*
Cobbing, Bob *64*
Cock, Stanley *6*
Cohen, David *69, 72*
Conner, Angela *94*

Coper, Hans *92*
Coutts-Smith, Kenneth *78*
Craddock, Kenneth *25*
Crowther, John *57*
Cundall, Charles *25*

D

Dacre, Winifred *90*
Dalou *66*
Dalwood, Hubert *39, 41, 45*
Davis, Harry *95*
Denvir, Bernard *40, 44*
De Stijl *67, 69, 70*
Dobson, Frank *25, 27*
Dugdale, T.C. *25*
Dunn, Allan *49, 94*

E

English, Stan *53*
Ernest, John *69, 70*

F

Fallon, Brian *92, 93*
Farrington, Christine *32*
Feiler, Paul *101*
Ferrari, Ivaldo *32*
Forbes, Stanhope *14*
Forrester, John *68*
Frink, Elizabeth *66*
Frost, Terry *18, 22, 98*
Fry, Roger *11*
Fry, Jeremy *40*

G

Gabo, Naum *40*
Gaudier-Brzeska *39*
Gerard, Alfred *83*
Giacometti, Alberto *27, 33*
Gilbert, H.C. *92*
Goedhuis, Michael *48*
Gonzalez *63, 103*
Gormley, Antony *78*
Graham-Dixon, Francis *76, 80*
Gropius, Walter *43*
Grose, Irving *4*

H

Hadley, Colin *42, 94*
Halkes, John *22*
Hammacher, A.M. *29*
Harrod, Tanya *95*

Hartung, Hans *27*
Hayes, Peter *92*
Hayman, Patrick *22*
Heath, Adrian *70*
Heath, Isobel *6*
Henderson, Ewen *92*
Hepworth, Barbara *6, 7, 9-13, 16,
     18, 22, 23, 24, 26, 28, 29, 30, 32,
     34, 35, 36, 38, 40, 43, 46, 48, 49,
     54, 55, 56, 63-67, 69, 70, 72, 73,
     75, 77, 83, 84, 89, 91-97*
Heron, Patrick *13, 14, 18, 30, 51, 93*
Hill, Anthony *70*
Hilton, Roger *36*
Hodin, J.P. *47, 48, 51*
Hornal, Bryan *58*
Hoskin, John *77, 96*

I
Illsley, Brian *40, 94*
Ingham, Margot *26*
Irwin, Bernard *92*

J
James, Philip *56*
Jason, Gillian *22*
Joyce, Max Wykes *92*

K
Kalman, Andras *26*
Kandinsky, Wassily *61, 68, 69, 83, 84*
Kennedy, R.C. *79*
Kenny, Michael *41*
Kestleman, Morris *80*
King, Philip *78, 79*
Kneale, Bryan *77*
Kollwitz, Kathe *26*

L
Lamb, Henry *25*
Lanyon, Peter *6, 30, 36, 64 , 98*
Leach, Bernard *10, 65, 95*
Leigh, Roger *6, 7, 22, 28, 53-62, 64,
     68, 70, 85, 99, 100, 101*
Leitch, Gwen *70*
Leonard, Charmian *7, 89*
Leonard, Keith *6, 28, 64, 83-90, 94*
Levy, Emmanuel *25*
Lewis, David *66*
Lim, Kim *78*
Lloyd Morgan, Conway *58*
Lowndes, Alan *25, 30*
Lowry, L.S. *25*
Lynton, Norbert *73, 76, 77, 78*

M
Maddox-Brown, Ford *26*
Maillol, *25, 27*
Major, Theodore *25*
Malevich, Kasimir *67, 68, 90*
Maltby, John *92*
Martin, Agnes *90*
Martin, Kenneth *70*
Martin, Leslie *43*
Martin, Mary *69*
Matisse, Henri *89, 93*
McWilliam, F.E. *25*
Mellis, Margaret *98*
Miles, June *103*
Milne, John *6, 7, 24-52, 55, 94, 96,
     100*
Mitchell, Denis *7, 8, 9-23, 28, 40,
     49, 50, 55, 64, 65, 70, 85, 91, 92,
     94, 96, 98, 100*
Mitchell, John *98*
Mondrian, Piet *39, 61, 63, 67-70,
     83, 84, 85*
Monet, Claude *93*
Moore, Henry *6, 9, 11, 25, 26, 27,
     53, 54, 55, 63, 64*
Moss, Marlow *69*
Mount, Paul *16, 101-104*
Mullins, Edwin *77*

N
Nalecz, Halima *70, 85*
Nance, Dicon *64, 94, 95, 96*
Nance, Robert Morton *95*
Nance, Robin *95*
Neubert, George *69*
Nicholson, Ben *6, 7, 10, 26, 27, 34,
     63, 64, 65, 70, 84, 90*
Nicholson, Jake *90*

O
O'Casey, Breon *22, 40, 91-93, 94,
     100*
O'Casey, Sean *91*
O'Malley, Tony *22, 36*

P
Parkinson, Peter *97*
Parr, Marjorie *13-16, 18, 37, 40, 43,
     44, 47, 48, 49, 51, 58, 92, 96*
Pascoe, Ernest *101*
Pasmore, Victor *70*
Pennie, Michael *58*
Pevsner *69*
Picasso, Pablo *26, 63, 93*

Piele, Misome *16, 70*
Pierce, Tom *94*
Plazzotta, Enzo *50*
Priestman, Jane *53*
Pye, William *72*

R
Ramsden, E.H. *51*
Rayner, Dirk *42, 94*
Read, Herbert *63, 84*
Reichardt, Jasia *81*
Richier, Germaine *66*
Robinson, E. *19*
Robertson, Bryan *15, 38, 39, 40, 41, 46, 47*
Rodewald, Cosmo *26, 27, 32, 34, 37, 44*
Rodin, A. *27, 66*
Rowe, Tommy *19, 20, 21, 23, 42, 49, 94, 96, 97*
Russell, John *77*
Rutherford, Harry *25*
Ryman, Robert *90*

S
Schlesinger, John *44*
Schuftan, K. *26*
Segal, Hyman *6*
Sellers, Stanley *34, 44*
Serra, Richard *74, 101*
Seuphor, Michel *66*
Singh, Reg *92*
Siroto, M. *26*
Skeaping, Paul *29*
Smith, Brian *37, 44, 95*
Smith, David *63, 103, 104*
Snow, Michael *22, 40, 69*
Somerville, Lilian *73*
Soulages *27*
Spencer, Charles *77, 81*
Startup, Peter *72*
Stevens, Jane *10*
Stocker, Norman *94, 96*
Stokes, Adrian *63*
Sutton, Keith *70*

T
Tait, T.S. *60*
Tatlin *100*
Taylor, Bruce *70*
Thursby, Peter *100, 101, 102*
Tribe, Barbara *16*
Turnbull, William *41, 72*

V
Vantongerloo *69*

W
Wakefield, Peter *59*
Walker, Richard *22*
Wall, Brian *6, 7, 28, 37, 63-82, 85, 94*
Wallis, Alfred *65*
Ward, Peter *96-98, 100*
Watson, Jacqui *95*
Wells, John *14, 18, 19, 21, 23, 30*
Whittet, G.S. *79*
Wilenski, R.H. *63*
Wilkinson, George *94, 95, 96*
Witkin, Isaac *78*
Wynter, Bryan *30, 40*

Z
Zadkine, Ossip *27, 84*